G.O.A.L Digga

Myra Sirrene

Imprint Productions, Inc.

G.O.A.L Digga

ISBN: 978-1-956884-16-6

Contributing Editor: All services completed by Imprint Productions, Inc.
Cover Design: All services completed by Imprint Productions, Inc.

Printed in the United States of America
Published by Imprint Productions, Inc.
First Edition 2023

Contact: **info@imprintproductionsinc.com**
Visit Us: **www.imprintproductionsinc.com**

Acknowledgements

I would like to take a moment to express my deepest appreciation and gratitude to the many people who have supported me in writing this book that challenges you to be efficient at goal structure.

First and foremost, I would like to thank my family and friends for the unwavering support and encouragement throughout the writing process. Your love and belief in me have been the fuel that kept me going, even during the toughest of times.

I am also grateful to the mentors and colleagues who have inspired and guided me on this journey. Your wisdom, insight, and expertise have been invaluable, and I could not have done this without you.

I would like to express my sincere gratitude to my publisher and editorial team Imprint
Productions Inc., who have worked tirelessly to bring this book to life. Your dedication, expertise, and attention to detail have insured that this book is of the highest quality.

I would also like to thank the many readers who have shared their feedback, sorrow, and insight with me along the way. Your input has helped me to share this book and ensure that it is relevant and meaningful to go to speak to structure their goals.

Last but not least, I would like to express my appreciation to all those who have supported me in ways big and small, whether through words of encouragement, acts of kindness, or simply by being there for me when I need it most.

Thank you all for your support and belief in me. This book is a product of our collective effort, and I could not have done it without you.

Dedication

I want to dedicate all the divine energy that it took for me to write this book to those individuals and aspiring entrepreneurs who have been doing the same thing over and over again and getting the same undesired results. You may be tired of getting the same outcomes and drawbacks out of life. Many of you have been starting over for years; you know, making those same New Year's Resolutions repeatedly. While others will get a little further, only to fall right back to where they started. Then there are those who get to where they thought they should be only to find out that is just a water drop of an ocean of possibilities.

This dedication is to all the underprivileged individuals who have lost hope and faith in their ability to set and achieve goals. I dedicate this book to those who may have faced immense hardship, discrimination, and/or poverty. Despite all the obstacles, you have the power to rise above it all and create the life you deserve.

It is important to set goals, as they provide direction, motivation, and a sense of purpose. They give you something to strive for and keep you focused on your dreams. Goals can be big or small, short-term, or long-term, but they are all equally important in shaping your life.

I want you to know that your past or current circumstances do not define you, nor do they limit your potential. You have the ability to achieve anything you set your mind to, as long as you believe in yourself and act towards your goals.

Remember, setting goals is not just about achieving materialistic success, but it is also about personal growth, self-improvement, and happiness. It is about creating a life that is meaningful and fulfilling to you. So, I urge you to take a step forward, set goals, and work towards achieving them. You are capable of creating the life that you desire, and I believe in you. This dedication is for you, who have lost hope but still have the power to make a change in your life. May you find strength, courage, and inspiration to set and achieve your goals.

That's the main reason why I wrote this book. I was all of the above! I was just like you. I was the Queen of writing or setting the same resolutions every year. I would do just enough to get by, but not enough to make an impact in my life. When I finally started to find my way past the "struggle bus," I was stuck at, What's next? Which way is it now? I see there is more ahead that I couldn't see before, but how do I get there? Now What?

What I found out was mind-boggling. I get it! I went from Homelessness to Home Ownership, which will be the title of my second book by the way, so look out for that. It will focus on finding your way to the American Dream a lot of us aim for! These are the simplest things in life, that once I thought, if only I learned this years ago, I would be further along in my success.

Does this sound familiar? Do you wake up each day, each month and each year repeating the same mistakes? If this is you, I want to applaud you for having the courage for change. Following the lessons in this book will get you to that next step and lead you to prosperity. I promise if you follow the principles in this book your next day, next month, and next year will be more intentional and bring you bigger results in your life and business.

Don't worry, I'm going over the skills that I have learned over the years, in this book; giving you the cheat codes to have the success you want out of your life.

I have now committed myself to assisting others in setting and accomplishing their goals. I'm teaching entrepreneurs how to start and brand their business as well as build generational wealth. I am a Serialpreneur. I have multiple streams of income, conduct multiple seminars, and coach and mentor others on accountability and goal structure. I also host my own podcast called Nubian Superstars Academy, where we bring the Superstars to you so that you can become *FINANCIALLY FREE!*

A goal without a plan is just a wish or desire. I want this book to be a resource that you can go back to as often as needed. I also want you to share this information with the people you care about so they can develop these same skills and go further in life. In dedicating this book to you, I want to challenge you to go after your dreams no matter the size of them. Use this book for your next 30-day challenge. Let it really soak in. Read one chapter per day and complete each action step. Always know your worth and never settle for less. If you don't stand for something, you will fall for anything. Above all, if no one else believes in you, know that I DO!

Destination: Success!

Welcome to the destination page of your journey for structured goal setting and achieving success in your personal and professional life. Congratulations on taking the first step for a more prosperous life.

As you journey through the pages of this book, you will discover how to set, structure, and achieve your goals with clarity and purpose. You will learn how to overcome common obstacles such as procrastination, self-doubt, and fear of failure, and develop a powerful mindset that will help you achieve lasting success.

To help you get the most out of your journey, I have provided a series of tools and exercises to help you apply the concepts in this book to your own life. These tools will help you clarify your vision, identify your core values, and set meaningful and achievable goals that are aligned with your purpose.

As you work through each chapter you will gain a deeper understanding of how to structure your goals or maximum impact. You will learn how to prioritize your goals, break them down into actionable steps, and track your progress to ensure you stay on track.

But this journey is not just about achieving your goals - it's also about personal growth and development. You would discover how to become more self-aware, develop new skills and competencies, and cultivate a growth mindset that will help you overcome challenges and achieve your full potential.

So buckle up and get ready for a transformational journey towards structured goal setting and achieving success in all aspects of your life. Whether you're looking to start your first business, improve your health, or strengthen your relationship, this book will provide you with the knowledge and tools you need to achieve your goals and live your best life. Let's get started!

Table of Contents

Get Ready!

Are you tired of setting goals but never achieving them? Do you struggle to stay motivated and focus on what really matters to you? If so my book is the solution you've been looking for.

In this practical and insightful guide, I provide readers with a clear and concise framework for structuring their goals and achieving success in all areas of life. Whether you're looking to advance your career, improve your health, or strengthen your relationships, my book will help you clarify your vision and take actionable steps for your desired outcomes.

Unlike other self-help books that offer vague advice and unrealistic promises, my approach is based on proven strategies and real-world experience. I draw on my own successes and failures, as well as the latest research in goal setting and personal development, to provide readers with a roadmap for achieving lasting change.

Throughout the book, I provide practical tools and exercises to help readers clarify their purpose, identify their core values, and prioritize their goals. I also share insights on overcoming common obstacles such as procrastination, self-doubt, and fear of failure, and offer guidance on how to stay motivated and focused on what really matters.

Whether you're a seasoned goal setter or just starting out on your personal development journey, my book will provide you with the knowledge and tools you need to achieve your goals and live your best life. So what are you waiting for? Let's plan your life today and take the G.O.A.L. Digga Challenge!

Introduction

G.O.A.L. Digga: You are going to become a sufficient G.O.A.L. (Generating an Objective and Ambitious Lifestyle) Digga after reading this book. The things you'll learn will give you the life skills needed for structuring and executing your goals, giving you a clear path to take action toward who you aspire to become.

I remember when I was 10 years young, not having a clear direction of who I wanted to be when I grew up. I wanted to become an actor, get married and have 10 children. But I didn't know if I truly wanted that, or just wanted to be like the people on the television. As a child I had an enormous imagination and it changed as often as the seasons, but I never stopped dreaming. Like many children where I came from, we didn't have many influencers to mentor us in the fields we wanted to pursue, or even give us a list of possibilities.

I must have been about 14 when I had access to a radio, and I listened to rap a lot and wanted to become a rapper. JJ Fad, Salt~n~Pepa, and Roxanne Shante were some of my favorites. I remember writing rhymes in my school notebook and holding my pencil as a mic, while I flowed. I seemed to always be getting in trouble for my creative expression which lowered my confidence and made me question my abilities, yet I held onto that dream.

That dream stayed with me into my mid-20's. I joined a rap group with a manager and everything. We did local gigs in surrounding cities. That career soon faded like my jeans; however, I still have bars!

I got married, had the children I wanted, living the "family life". I learned to cook, clean, wash hair, help with schoolwork, and repeat. I've worked many underpaid jobs with long hours. I was even introduced to entrepreneurship for the first time and started my first business, a restaurant named "Big Mama's HotPot" which failed in 8 months. I thought "What happened to my aspirations? Was I to do this the rest of my life?" Don't get me wrong, I love my children and would do anything for them, I just remembered there has to be more to life than this. I wanted more in my life.

I started off with making those New Year's Resolutions, like we tend to do. You know the ones we start the first week of January and by the second or third week of that same month we promise ourselves to start in February. We continue to procrastinate till it's O.V., a little saying we used to say in school for it being over before it started, for those that's not familiar with Ebonics. Wait, or maybe that's just slang. Anyways, the point is, I was now writing down things I wanted to get done or things I wished to have that year.

After doing this for some years, I accomplished some resolutions and fell through on others, but it still wasn't making an impact in my life. Now I know why, it was because I still didn't know what I wanted. One resolution I continued to make was, get another car. I usually did that every tax season only because I would buy a lemon with cash. A lemon, by the way, is a car you buy for what you thought was a good deal, only to find out every month you have to put it in the shop to fix something. Another one was, get a good job, as I stated before, I went through some jobs.

A third one was, exercise more, now that's a resolution that I accomplished. Well, I did have youth and good genes on my side, so I really didn't have to do much exercise then.

Now, I eventually landed a pretty good job working for Navistar. I was working temporarily at first, but I worked hard and was hired permanently. I even worked my way up for a team leader position where I was responsible for about 13 employees. Wow, a sista was coming up, bringing home $1800 a week! That was a lot of money in 2010 in Huntsville, Alabama before the cost of living skyrocketed because of gentrification. Best of all, I purchased a 2005 GMC Yukon Denali long body SUV, no more lemons for me! Now, remember me mentioning getting far in life only to fall back? Well, that's what happened to me. Bad decisions lead to bad consequences. That's a whole 'nother book and will be my third one, I may tweak the name though. Moving on!

"I'm still anxious to know what I'm doing wrong, and yet I can't find the answers." Now mind you, I got my first computer around 2006, it was a used one that my mom gave to my children to use for schoolwork. The only thing I saw them use it for was Myspace by the way. I had no knowledge of the World Wide Web or the wealth of information that I could have connected with. Remember I was a Homemaker, separated by now, raising 6 active children at this time.

Everyone going to bed on time was my resolution at this point. Something inside of me still longed for change and a better life, especially now that I have children that depend on me. And eventually having my first 2 grandchildren two years later.

It was after my eighth child was a few months away from turning 3 in 2013, when I found myself homeless for about the fifth time, that I had a sense of urgency to conquer this curse that I alone created for myself. Now, I could say it was my environment that I was in, that made me do it, but you didn't hear that from me. Nonetheless, I did pack up everything I could fit in my Denali truck including my 5 children that were still living with me, my 3 adult children had their own living arrangements, and everything else I put in storage. Which I later lost because I couldn't afford to make the payments anymore.

I didn't know where we were going or where we would end up. Wait, I did know, I looked up some shelters near me, but wanted the furthest one away from Huntsville. I found one in Florence, Alabama, about 80 miles away, and I called that one. Luckily for me the shelter had space available for all of us. At least we had a roof over our heads. I was determined to make a new start for my children and myself. So, I started making vision boards, writing down my goals, and became a sufficient G.O.A.L. Digga.

What you're going to find in this book: G.O.A.L. Digga, is, first and foremost, how to shift your mindset. The way you think is essential to who you'll become. The way you think will drive your actions in life, which will eventually determine what happens in your life. Next, you're going to learn how to hold yourself accountable, how to stay committed, and be aware of the costs. Finally, you will be able to plan your vision, set effective and measurable goals, and execute to that desired lifestyle you've always wanted.

The point I'm making is this, when creating your goals, you must be a G.O.A.L. Digga:

G - Generate. To generate is to cause, to arise, or come about. In other words, you want to create it by writing it down.

O - Objective. Now that you have a clear goal, you can be specific about its objective or the effort to attain it.

A - Ambitious. You have to possess a strong desire and determination to achieve it.

L - Lifestyle. The way in which you choose to live.

What is a G.O.A.L. Digga? G.O.A.L. Digga = A person who creates and executes goals to gain prosperity.

Setting Personal Goals...... and Seeing Them Though

"Change will not come if we wait for some other person or some other time. We are the ones we've been waiting for. We are the change we seek." – Barack Obama

Setting goals and seeing them through is an essential skill for success in any aspect of life. Whether it's personal, professional, or academic goals, having a clear vision and a plan of action can help you achieve what you set out to accomplish. In this book, we will discuss some key points to keep in mind when setting goals and seeing them through.

The first step to setting and achieving goals is to identify what you want to accomplish. Whether it's a short-term or long-term goal, it's important to have a clear idea of what you're striving for. Once you have a goal in mind, write it down and be specific about what you want to achieve. This will help you stay focused and committed to your goal.

Next, break down your goal into smaller, manageable tasks. This will help you stay motivated and give you a sense of progress as you work towards your larger goal. It's also important to set deadlines for yourself, so you have a timeline to work within.

One of the most important things you can do to see your goals through is to stay committed. This means dedicating time and effort towards your goal, even when you face obstacles or setbacks. Keep in mind that setbacks are a normal part of the process and use them as an opportunity to learn and grow.

Another important factor in seeing your goals through is to stay organized. Keep track of your progress and adjust your plan as needed. This will help you stay focused and motivated, and it will also help you identify areas where you may need to put in more effort.

It's also important to surround yourself with positive influences. Seek out friends, family, or mentors who will support and encourage you as you work towards your goals. This can make a big difference in keeping you motivated and on track. You always want to stay accountable. This means holding yourself responsible for your progress and being honest about any challenges or setbacks you face. You can also seek out an accountability partner or coach to help keep you on track.

When achieving your goals, you want to be flexible. Be open to adjusting your plan as needed and be willing to try new approaches if something isn't working. This can help you stay motivated and focused on your goal.

It's also important to celebrate your successes along the way. Whether it's a small milestone or a major accomplishment, take time to acknowledge your progress and feel proud of what you've achieved. This can help you stay motivated and committed to seeing your goal through to the end.

Remember that achieving your goals is a journey, not a destination. Be patient with yourself, stay committed to your goal, and keep moving forward even when you face challenges. With dedication, perseverance, and a clear plan of action, you can achieve anything you set your mind to.

Serena Williams, a legendary tennis player who set specific goals and achieved remarkable success throughout her career. From a young age, Serena and her sister Venus Williams were introduced to tennis by their father, Richard Williams. Recognizing their immense talent and potential, Richard set clear and specific goals for Serena's tennis career. He believed that both his daughters would become world-class tennis players and win multiple Grand Slam titles.

Serena embraced her father's vision and worked tirelessly to make it a reality. She set specific goals for herself, such as becoming the number one ranked player in the world and winning all four Grand Slam tournaments. Serena's dedication and determination were evident from an early age as she trained rigorously and competed in tournaments around the world.

In 1999, at the age of 17, Serena won her first Grand Slam title, defeating Martina Hingis in the final of the U.S. Open. This victory marked the beginning of a remarkable career filled with numerous accomplishments and records. Serena went on to win a total of 23 Grand Slam singles titles, the most by any player in the Open Era.

Throughout her career, Serena remained focused and specific with her goals. She set records, achieved a "Career Grand Slam" by winning all four major tournaments, and dominated the tennis world with her powerful playing style and unwavering determination. Despite facing injuries, setbacks, and fierce competition, Serena consistently pushed herself to reach new heights and surpass her own expectations.

Beyond her on-court achievements, Serena became a role model and inspiration to many for her resilience, strength, and unwavering belief in herself. She shattered stereotypes and broke barriers, becoming a powerful advocate for equality and women's empowerment.

Serena Williams' story is a testament to the power of setting specific goals and working relentlessly towards them. Through her unwavering focus and determination, she became one of the greatest tennis players of all time. Her story reminds us that with clarity, dedication, and perseverance, we can overcome obstacles and achieve extraordinary success in our chosen endeavours.

If you ever dreamed of the perfect life, this book is for you. You'll discover how setting personal goals can help you achieve the life you always wanted - and deserve. It's imperative to plan your life. The tools that you learn in this book will guide you through a simple, powerful, and effective system for setting and achieving goals. Using this method will help you start from nothing and achieve extraordinary success.

This book will save you years of hard work and help you get ahead faster. It will help you to achieve the goals that are most important to you. The biggest takeaway I want you to receive from reading this book is, write down your goals, make plans to achieve them, and work on your plans every single day. If you follow that concept, it will be more valuable to you than any degree you obtain. For it takes these very skills to get you those credentials. It will change your life, it changed mine.

Without goals you're just drifting through life, accepting anything that comes your way. With goals you aim at your target and hit it. After reading this book you will have the knowledge and power needed to strive and not take anything for granted. You will also be able to create your own reality. When you've made decisions in the past, it probably was a good idea based on the knowledge that you had. Now knowing what you are learning from this book, you'll acknowledge that the choices you made would've been different with this new mindset.

You don't have to be a rocket scientist to become a G.O.A.L. Digga. All you need is dreams, hopes, and desires; to have, do, and be. What are your dreams? What are the hopes that you have? What type of desires in life do you want? What are the things you want to have? What would you love to do? Who do you want to be? What do you foresee for your finances, your family, and your health? This is the foundation of goal setting.

It's important to know exactly what you want to achieve and the period of time it'll take to manifest that achievement. With clarity comes concentrated effort and an ability to weed out diverting distractions. According to Edwin Locke's famous Goal Setting Theory, "the more challenging and specific a goal, the more likely it will be achieved." So, think BIG!

This book will also guide you to creating results through focus, commitment, and accountability. By mastering these skills, it will enable you to transform your lifestyle and create your own reality. You can unlock secrets that are simple to implement, to help you accomplish more in less time. It all boils down to you, are you sick and tired of being sick and tired?

You just have to have a plan. It's no different than planning a trip out of town. You map out the directions to know the route to take along the way, you plan to stop by nearby gas stations to refuel and take bathroom breaks, and depending how far you go, you may have to stop for refreshments. Those are the obstacles. All of that has to be considered when planning a trip, not to mention the cost as well.

You'll gain the confidence you need to execute and ensure those goals are seen through. This is not something that you can just set and forget. You'll have to put in the action plan that it takes to make this happen. Are you going to be a walker or a talker?

Time is too valuable to be wasted. Take back control of your time. Create your reality. I want you to be a walker, and with each step you take, it will lead you to prosperity. Setting goals will boost your self-confidence and help you discover the meaning and purpose of your life. It'll propel you into action and seeing your progress will give you great satisfaction.

With each chapter, you'll have action steps to take, that will get you closer to your G.O.A.L. Digga status. Always remember to reward yourself with each milestone you cross.

I too want to reward you as well for making the first step in taking control of your life, by sending you a free G.O.A.L. Digga T-shirt. Make a post of you holding your G.O.A.L. Digga Book on your social media pages and tag me on my Instagram page (g.o.a.l.digga) and I'll send you a free t-shirt to wear on your journey.

A great addition to this book is my G.O.A.L. Digga Journal. The purpose of the journal is for you to write down your ideas, to brainstorm, and to complete your action steps. Your Journal is going to have your rough draft or blueprint of your goals. You would then transfer your plans from your journal over to your G.O.A.L. Digga Planner.

Your G.O.A.L. Digga Planner is structured in a way for you to complete your goals quarterly, every 12 weeks. Some of your goals will be done before that which is great. But those bigger goals you want to get done within a 12-week time frame. If you want to start a restaurant this year, I'm not saying you'll get that done in 12 weeks. What I'm saying is every 12 weeks you have a different goal to get you closer to that end goal. For instance, the first 12 weeks may be to incorporate your business and write a business plan. The next 12 weeks may be to establish funding, and another 12 weeks, looking for a building. You keep going until your goal is reached.

Action Steps

To get the most out of this book, head over to our website, www.goaldigga.org and purchase your G.O.A.L. Digga Planner along with your G.O.A.L. Digga Journal. Also get free guide templates that are printable to help you along the way. Join the community of G.O.A.L. Diggas on YouTube, Facebook, Instagram, Twitter, TikTok, Clubhouse, and Snapchat so you can share your story and inspire others. What better way to hold yourself accountable by sharing your journey?

"My Mission in Life is not merely to Survive, but to Thrive; and to do so with some Passion, some Compassion, some Humor, and some Style." – Maya Angelo

1

Abundance is Yours

Having abundance in life means having an abundance of happiness, love, fulfillment, and prosperity. It's about living a life of abundance in all areas, not just material wealth. In this chapter, we will discuss some key points to keep in mind when striving for abundance in life.

The first step to achieving abundance in life is to focus on the positive. This means looking for good in every situation and finding joy in the small things. When you focus on the positive, you attract more positivity into your life, creating a cycle of abundance.

Next, it's important to set intentions for abundance. This means setting clear goals and visualizing yourself living a life of abundance. When you set clear intentions and visualize your desired outcome, you open yourself up to opportunities and possibilities that align with your goals.

Another key factor in achieving abundance in life is to practice gratitude. This means being thankful for what you already have, and appreciating the abundance that already exists in your life. When you practice gratitude, you attract more abundance into your life, creating a positive cycle of abundance.

It's also important to cultivate a positive mindset. This means adopting a can-do attitude and believing that anything is possible. When you have a positive mindset, you open yourself up to new opportunities and possibilities, creating a path towards abundance.

Another important factor in achieving abundance in life is to let go of limiting beliefs. This means identifying and releasing negative thoughts and beliefs that may be holding you back from living a life of abundance. When you let go of limiting beliefs, you create space for new opportunities and possibilities to enter your life.

It's also important to take action towards your goals. This means taking steps towards achieving your desired outcome, and being proactive in creating the life you want. When you take action towards your goals, you create momentum and move towards abundance.

Another key factor in achieving abundance in life is to surround yourself with positive influences. This means surrounding yourself with people who uplift and inspire you, and avoiding those who bring negativity into your life. When you surround yourself with positivity, you create an environment that supports abundance.

It's also important to take care of yourself. This means prioritizing self-care, and taking care of your physical, mental, and emotional wellbeing. When you take care of yourself, you create a foundation for abundance to thrive.

Another important factor in achieving abundance in life is to be open to receiving. This means being open to receiving love, support, and opportunities that align with your goals. When you are open to receiving, you create a flow of abundance in your life.

Remember that abundance is a state of mind. It's about living a life of abundance in all areas, not just material wealth. By focusing on the positive, setting intentions, practicing gratitude, cultivating a positive mindset, letting go of limiting beliefs, taking action, surrounding yourself with positivity, taking care of yourself, being open to receiving, and adopting a mindset of abundance, you can live a life of abundance in all areas.

An inspiring story of abundance and what that can look like is the story of Oprah Winfrey. Oprah was born into poverty in rural Mississippi in 1954. She faced numerous challenges in her early years, including a difficult upbringing and a tumultuous family life. Despite these hardships, Oprah possessed an innate curiosity, intelligence, and a strong desire to succeed.

At a young age, Oprah discovered her passion for storytelling and communication. She began her career in the media as a radio host and later transitioned to television. In 1986, she launched "The Oprah Winfrey Show," a daytime talk show that quickly became a sensation. Through her authenticity, empathy, and ability to connect with people from all walks of life, Oprah captivated audiences and inspired millions around the world.

"The Oprah Winfrey Show" became the highest-rated talk show in television history, earning Oprah fame and fortune. She used her platform to address important social issues, promote personal growth, and advocate for the underprivileged. Oprah's impact extended beyond television, as she launched her own media empire, Harpo Productions, and became one of the most influential figures in the entertainment industry.

Oprah's success in the media was just the beginning of her journey to abundance. She expanded her ventures to include publishing, founding her book club that propelled numerous authors to bestseller status. She also ventured into acting, producing, and philanthropy. One of Oprah's notable achievements was the establishment of the Oprah Winfrey Leadership Academy for Girls in South Africa. This academy provides educational opportunities to underprivileged girls, empowering them to break free from the cycle of poverty and become leaders in their communities.

Oprah's story is a testament to the power of resilience, determination, and the pursuit of one's passions. She overcame adversity, transformed her life, and used her success to uplift others. Her journey from a poverty-stricken childhood to becoming a billionaire media mogul and a globally recognized philanthropist is an inspiration to countless individuals around the world. Her story proves that with hard work, perseverance, and a belief in oneself, it is possible to turn dreams into reality and achieve abundance.

What does abundance mean to you? As defined: to have an abundance of something is to have more than you need or a very large quantity of something. Such as an abundance of wealth is having an unlimited supply of cash. In other words, you have plenty of. A plethora of. An extremely plentiful or over sufficient quantity or supply.

Now that you know what abundance is, how can you apply it to your everyday life? You want to know the right question to ask yourself. You want to relearn how to think, with an end goal in mind. You want to be able to unlock your subconscious power. You also want to have a clear vision. And set a strategic action plan in the form of setting goals.

First you have to reset and change the way you think. What belief system can you evict to create space? You can only carry so much. You have to make room for abundance. Stop holding onto limiting thoughts. You have to let go of your limited way of thinking. For example: I can't lose weight. I don't have enough money. I'm shy. I've always been this way. I don't know how to make more money. Let's dismantle this truth in your mind. Let's think differently.

Start building a belief system around having a "How Can I" mindset. For example: How can I lose weight? How can I earn more money? How can I win friends and influence people? How can I get out of my comfort zone and be comfortable with being uncomfortable? How can I start my own business and become an entrepreneur? It may be difficult at first because you're conditioned to use negative thoughts. It's OK, the more you implement your new way of thinking, the easier it gets. As long as you identify when you have those negative thoughts and turn them around immediately, you'll create a habit of switching that negative switch off.

I mentioned being homeless before, right? The more that I achieve, the more I want to succeed. I didn't just stop at getting an apartment, I want to own my own home. I didn't stop at getting the perfect career, I want to create my own financial stability. I want to be in control of my time. I want to be able to go where I want to go, do the things that I want to do, whenever I want to do them. I want to live in abundance and prosperity. So, I continue to build and continue to grow.

As a G.O.A.L. Digga, we accept having abundance, we embrace having abundance, and we generate abundance. We understand with each no there is still a yes. We plan, we execute, we evaluate, and we adjust. We predict obstacles and maneuver through them. We are aware of the associated cost. Lastly, we take action and commit to consistency.

Take control of your thoughts. If you haven't watched the movie "The Secret" a 2006 film by Rhonda Byrne, I highly suggest you do. It is based on the belief of the pseudoscientific law of attraction, which claims that thoughts can change a person's life directly. The book alleges energy as assurance of its effectiveness. I can personally say that I have applied this concept to my everyday life and have been successful at shifting my mindset in how I think and how I speak.

Unlock your potential. If you had the ability to achieve any goal you could ever set for yourself, what would it be? What would you have? What would you do? Identify what gives you the greatest sense of meaning and purpose. How can you have that? We all know it's not where you start – it's how you finish.

"Unlearn those thoughts that have gotten you the outcome that you don't deserve and relearn the strategies that will lead you to prosperity." – Myra Sirrene

Action Steps

Now that you have taken the first action steps, and you now have ordered your G.O.A.L. Digga Planner and G.O.A.L. Digga Journal. Take out your G.O.A.L. Digga Journal and write down what abundance looks like for you. Write down an Aspirational Vision for yourself. Don't overthink it, just write things that you want to have, places you want to go, things you want to do, and the person you want to be. The sky's the limit. Be creative! Think BIG! Are you ready for abundance?

"I was willing to completely die to any form of me that I have been so that I can be the woman that I was becoming. The reason why a lot of people won't become who they want is because they're too attached to who they've been."
– Lisa Nichols

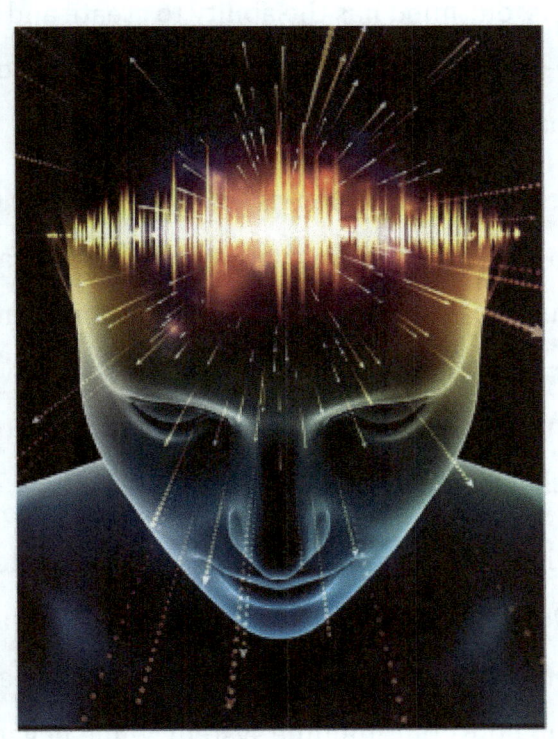

2

The Power of the Mind

The mind is a powerful tool that can shape our reality and influence the course of our lives. From our thoughts to our beliefs, our mind has the ability to create and manifest what we desire. In this chapter, we will discuss some key points that highlight the power of the mind.

The first key point to note is that the mind has the power to influence our emotions. Our thoughts can shape our emotions, and our emotions can influence our behavior. By controlling our thoughts, we can have a better understanding of our emotions and take control of our behavior.

The mind has the power to influence our physical health. Our thoughts and beliefs can have a profound impact on our physical health. Positive thoughts and beliefs can boost our immune system, while negative thoughts can weaken it.

We have the power to manifest our desires. Our thoughts and beliefs can shape our reality and manifest what we desire. By focusing on positive thoughts and beliefs, we can attract positive outcomes in our lives.

Another key point is that our mind has the power to influence our relationships. Our thoughts and beliefs can shape our interactions with others and influence the dynamics of our relationships. By cultivating positive thoughts and beliefs, we can create harmonious and fulfilling relationships.

We can overcome challenges. Our thoughts and beliefs can help us overcome obstacles and challenges in our lives. By focusing on positive thoughts and beliefs, we can find solutions to problems and move forward.

There are no limits to what we are capable of. We have the ability to increase our creativity. Our thoughts and beliefs can influence our creativity and help us come up with innovative ideas and solutions. By cultivating positive thoughts and beliefs, we can tap into our creative potential.

Our mind can increase our productivity. Our thoughts and beliefs can influence our motivation and drive and help us achieve our goals. By focusing on positive thoughts and beliefs, we can increase our productivity and achieve more in less time.

Is it confidence that you're after? Guess what, we can increase our confidence. Our thoughts and beliefs can shape our self-image and influence our confidence levels. By cultivating positive thoughts and beliefs, we can increase our confidence and self-esteem.

Our mind can also increase our resilience. Our thoughts and beliefs can help us bounce back from setbacks and challenges. By focusing on positive thoughts and beliefs, we can develop resilience and overcome adversity.

We are truly amazing beings; the mind has the power to bring us peace and happiness. Our thoughts and beliefs can shape our perception of the world and influence our sense of peace and happiness. By cultivating positive thoughts and beliefs, we can find inner peace and happiness.

The power of the mind is immense. By cultivating positive thoughts and beliefs, we can shape our reality, overcome challenges, increase our productivity, creativity, and confidence, and find peace and happiness. The mind is a powerful tool that we can use to create the life we desire.

In order to get to the abundance that you seek, again you must first have a mindset shift. Before setting any kind of goal you have to get your mind right. When you know more you do more. When you do more, you get more. When you get more, you'll be closer to abundance.

Think of things you've never thought of before. Say things you've never said before. Do things you've never done before. Go places you've never gone before. Talk to people you've never talked to before. Remember if you want a different lifestyle you have to live differently.

Don't forget that G.O.A.L. Digga status! We Generate an Objective and Ambitious Lifestyle. We know that actions deliver results, we stick to the plan, and we understand that it's a process. We measure what's working versus what does not work and make informed decisions. We execute by all means necessary. We also utilize our time intentionally.

Someone who used the power of their mind to achieve success is the story of Dr. Wayne Dyer. Wayne Dyer was born in Detroit, Michigan, in 1940, and faced a challenging childhood marked by poverty and family discord. Despite these circumstances, Dyer developed a deep interest in self-help and personal development from an early age. He realized that he had the power to shape his own reality through his thoughts and beliefs.

Dyer pursued higher education and earned a doctorate in educational counselling, focusing his research on the power of the mind and the impact of thoughts on personal transformation. He began his career as a college professor, but soon realized that his true calling was to share his knowledge and insights with a wider audience.

In the 1970s, Dyer published his first book, *Your Erroneous Zones*, which became an instant bestseller. The book explored the concept of self-limiting beliefs and provided practical guidance on how to overcome them. Dyer's message resonated with readers who were seeking guidance and empowerment in their own lives.

Building upon his initial success, Dyer went on to write numerous other bestselling books, including *The Power of Intention*, *Manifest Your Destiny*, and *Change Your Thoughts - Change Your Life*. Through his writing and lectures, Dyer inspired millions of people to tap into the power of their minds and transform their lives.

One of Dyer's key teachings was the importance of shifting one's perspective and adopting a positive mindset. He emphasized that our thoughts and beliefs shape our reality, and by cultivating empowering thoughts, we can manifest success, happiness, and abundance. Dyer encouraged individuals to take responsibility for their own lives, empowering them to create the reality they desired through the power of their minds.

Dyer's impact extended beyond his books and lectures. He appeared on television shows, conducted workshops and seminars, and became a prominent figure in the self-help and personal development community. His teachings inspired countless individuals to overcome adversity, achieve their goals, and lead more fulfilling lives.

Throughout his career, Dyer remained committed to spreading his message of personal empowerment and spiritual growth. He touched the lives of millions through his work, and his legacy continues to inspire people around the world even after his passing in 2015.

Wayne Dyer's story is a testament to the transformative power of the mind. Through his teachings and personal examples, he showed that by harnessing the power of our thoughts and beliefs, we can overcome obstacles, achieve success, and create a life of purpose and fulfillment. His story serves as a reminder that our minds have the incredible capacity to shape our reality, and with the right mindset, we can truly achieve greatness.

We all have the power to decide the type of person we wish to be, which is when we use our conscious mind, making a conscious decision. For instance: If I wanted to become a doctor, I would go to college and get the credentials and degrees that are necessary to become one. If I wanted to become a lawyer, I would go to law school and do the same thing. When I'm hungry, I get something to eat. When I'm dirty, I bathe.

However, the subconscious mind is responsible for success and is ultimately programmed by our thoughts and beliefs. Every experience, conditions, and acts are the reactions to your thoughts that you have and have been the reactions of your subconscious mind. It's what you believe in your own mind that gives you that result. You tell yourself that you can't achieve something, and you believe that to be true. Like that saying that states: whether you think you can or think you can't you're probably right. You have to own it.

We can influence our reality depending on how we feed it. When thinking there's a cause and an effect. That's why it's essential that we take charge of our thoughts. The universe is putting everything and all conditions in place for that thought to come true. The subconscious mind does not reason or think for itself; it simply follows the orders we consciously input. Your subconscious mind is amenable to suggestion.

How you get ahead in life is determined by what you think of yourself, your own thoughts. You become what you think about most of the time. Whatever you think about the most, positive, or negative will become your reality. Successful people think about what they want and how to get it most of the time. Unhappy, unsuccessful people think about what they don't want most of the time. Remember energy grows where energy goes.

I'll give you an example. I remember about 4 years ago I was living in the country, and I would frequently see spiders, and I was always frightened that a spider would be in my shoe when I put on my shoes. That thought alone put everything in place to make it happen. One day while dumping my shoe, because I always did that just in case a spider was in there. One day it happened, a spider jumped out. So, you see it was me, my thoughts, and the universe that put it all together and made it come true.

Identify what you are currently thinking. Be aware of what you say to yourself. For instance, stop telling yourself you can't do it, you don't have it, you don't know how. Because rest assured that is exactly what you'll get. Nothing! Be as detailed as possible when assessing your life. You have to control your thoughts right now, in order to get to where you want to be. What do you think right now? What do you tell yourself right now? What are your actions that you are doing right now?

I'm still not perfect at it. However, like a light switch I know how to turn it off. When those negative thoughts get into my mind, I flip it around and start speaking positive messages. I have to give my subconscious mind the correct orders to follow, so it can give me the outcome that I desire. Your subconscious mind and your conscious mind must be aligned. You can't expect to get the results that you need just by thinking about it. You have to know it can happen as well.

When you think about that thing you want you have to know it's attainable when you speak it. You have to see yourself there receiving it.

It's like a pregnancy. When you first get the news that you're having a baby, you know the outcome is that baby being here, right? So, what do you do? Do you sit around and contemplate the outcome of the pregnancy before you prepare for it? No. You start now to prepare for that baby. You buy clothes, crib, you think of boy and girl names, you even have a baby shower and invite all your friends and family who bring you gifts. Everything is lined up for that end result, the "Baby". You know it's not here yet but, in about nine months you'll expect it.

Have that same energy about your life and your future. We have adopted a way of thinking. A negative way of thinking. We have been trained to have that thought process. Don't you remember being told that money doesn't grow on trees? Or if you wanted to go to a restaurant and your parents asked you if you had some restaurant money? We weren't taught how to think like successful people do. We weren't taught how to use our subconscious mind. For that matter to even know what that means.

Action Steps

Now, I want you to take out that same G.O.A.L. Digga Journal and write down ways you can change your mindset. Write down a positive way of thinking versus the way you used to think now that you have the tools to unlock your subconscious mind. Practice turning that negative switch off daily and implementing a different way of thinking about yourself. It's going to take consistency, the more that you think better, the better you'll become at mastering this process. Are you ready for a clearer mind?

"Bring your best to the moment, then, whether it fails or succeeds, at least you know you gave all you had. We need to live the best that's in us." – Angela Bassett

3
Letting Go of Fear

"I have learned over the years that when one's mind is made up, this diminishes fear; knowing what must be done does away with fear" – Rosa Parks

What is fear? Fear is an unpleasant emotion caused by the belief that someone or something is dangerous, likely to cause pain, or a threat. Fear plays an important part in our lives when we're creating goals. You may have a fear of failing, so you write down a goal that's super easy. Or you may have a fear that the goal is too high, and you don't have the confidence that you need to execute it. Either way it's important for us to conquer that fear.

I'm not sure where I heard this from, however, "it goes a little some-mm like this"; The fear of pain is worse than the pain itself. Let me give you an example of that. During summer when the bees and wasps are out. A lot of us do not want to get stung, so at the sight of one we run, waving our arms, and screeching. That fear of getting stung and how much it would hurt is all we think about. But when stung we realize, although it hurts, it's not as painful as the fear of getting hurt.

We often give up on our goals before we even begin. Why do you think that is? It's the fear! That thought in your mind is saying it's too hard, you can't do it, you don't know what to do, you don't have time, it's going to take too long. So, you're scared to fail. You're scared of what people think. You don't want to disappoint yourself. You don't want to work hard for it. You put up all those roadblocks. You are holding you back.

A G.O.A.L. Digga "successful people " we fail more than unsuccessful people because we attempt it over and over and over again. We do whatever it takes to keep our promises we've made to ourselves. Commitment is vital and builds trust and strong relationships with others. When we keep promises, it builds self-confidence and shows what character we express. The bottom line is we stay committed and do whatever it takes to succeed. We are fearless.

A person who let go of fear and accomplished their desires, is the story of Arunima Sinha. Arunima is the first female amputee to climb Mount Everest, the highest peak in the world.

Arunima was a national level volleyball player who aspired to join the Indian Police Service (IPS). One day in 2011, while traveling by train to take an exam for the IPS, she was attacked by a group of men who tried to snatch her gold chain. When she resisted, they pushed her out of the train, and she fell onto the tracks, where another train ran over her legs. She lost one leg and the other was severely injured, which ultimately had to be amputated.

The accident left Arunima devastated, but she did not give up on life. Instead, she set her sights on a new goal – to climb Mount Everest. She was determined to prove to herself and the world that she was capable of achieving her dreams, despite her disability.

Arunima faced many challenges on her journey to climb Mount Everest. She had to train hard for months to build her strength and endurance. She also had to overcome her fear of climbing and the dangers that come with it, such as altitude sickness, frostbite, and avalanches.

But Arunima did not let her fear hold her back. She climbed smaller peaks to gain experience and build her confidence. She also received support from her family, friends, and the Indian government, who provided her with funding and equipment for the climb.

In April 2013, Arunima set out to climb Mount Everest with a team of sherpas and other climbers. Despite facing many obstacles, including harsh weather conditions and low oxygen levels, she did not give up. She climbed for several days, braving the cold and the altitude, until she finally reached the summit on May 21, 2013.

Arunima's achievement inspired many people around the world, especially those with disabilities. She showed that with determination, hard work, and courage, anything is possible, and that we should not let our fears or limitations hold us back from pursuing our dreams.

Today, Arunima continues to inspire and motivate others. She has written several books and gives motivational talks to encourage people to overcome their fears and achieve their goals. Her story is a testament to the power of the human spirit and the importance of letting go of fear to accomplish our desires.

If you think in terms of solutions, you can eliminate fear. Don't think of the difficulties of how to do something, or the problems that you're having. Think about a solution on how to overcome that obstacle. Think of how to get through that challenge, and what steps to take. Solution-oriented people usually ask, "How can we solve this?" Then we take action to execute. We have no time to complain or dwell about what caused the problem, or how angry we are and how unfortunate it is.

Problem solving should be a skill that you learn like when you drive a car or ride a bike. The more you do it the easier it should be. As you do it over and over again, you become better at it and eventually there's no problem that you can't solve. As you set your goals, it will become second nature to have a contingency plan in place to assist with your outcome of success. Remember you're letting that fear of being stung by that bee or wasp prevent you from relaxing in the sun. When in reality that wasp can care less about you as long as you're not around its nest or threatening it.

I think it's safe to say, you can eliminate your fear by simply learning the skill set to solve problems. That is exactly how I learned to conquer my fears, and still implement them today. Whenever an obstacle arises or I see a potential setback, I think of the next best solution. I think of how I can make this work. I think of who I hire to take care of this? I think of what the sacrifices are I need to make?

I cannot stress enough on how consistency is the key to success. For instance, since being in my mid 40s I noticed I have to work at staying in shape as I see myself. I could no longer rely on my youth to keep my body, mind, and spirit fit. If I want my vessel to take care of me I have to take care of my vessel.

I had to change my habits. I could no longer consume the food I wanted to eat at the time I wanted to eat. Especially now with not knowing exactly what's even in the food we consume. I know "Black don't crack but it can get Phat." Everyone has their own perception of what that is, all I'm saying is for me, at 5 '3 in height, to keep my weight at 160 lbs., which I'm comfortable with, I have to be consistent with my weight goals.

Fear is a powerful emotion that can hold us back from achieving our goals and living our lives to the fullest. It can manifest in different forms, such as fear of failure, fear of rejection, fear of the unknown, and many others. However, holding onto fear can be detrimental to our mental and emotional wellbeing, and it can limit our potential. Therefore, it's important to learn how to let go of fear and move forward in life with courage and confidence.

Here are six tips for letting go of fear:

1. Identify the source of your fear: Understanding the root cause of your fear can help you to address it more effectively. Is it a past experience that has left a lasting impact? Or is it something that you imagine might happen in the future? Once you know what triggers your fear, you can begin to work on it.

2. Acknowledge your fear: Don't try to suppress or ignore your fear. Instead, acknowledge it and accept that it's a natural human emotion. It's okay to be afraid sometimes, but it's not okay to let it control your life.

3. Challenge your fears: When you face your fears head-on, you'll realize that they're not as big and scary as you thought. Take small steps to challenge your fears, such as speaking in public, taking a new course, or asking someone out. Each time you face your fears, you'll build up your confidence and resilience.

4. Focus on the present moment: Fear often arises from worries about the future or regrets about the past. However, you can only control the present moment. By focusing on the here and now, you can reduce anxiety and worry about what might happen.

5. Practice self-care: Taking care of your physical, mental, and emotional health can help you to manage your fears. Get enough sleep, eat a healthy diet, exercise regularly, and spend time doing things that make you happy.

6. Seek support: It's okay to ask for help when you're struggling with fear. Talk to someone you trust, such as a friend, family member, or therapist. They can offer you guidance and support as you work through your fears.

Letting go of fear is a process that takes time and effort. But by facing your fears, challenging them, and taking care of yourself, you can overcome them and live a more fulfilling life. Remember, fear is just a feeling, and it doesn't have to control your life.

Action Steps

Take out that G.O.A.L. Digga Journal again. This time write down all of the fear factors that are holding you back, the ones you think are standing in your way. I want you to be honest with yourself. No need to dress it up, you can't fool yourself. This is the perfect time to really dive in to see who you are and where to begin. This is important for your growth, going into the next chapter where you will turn that fear into a magnetizing positive energy source. Are you ready to become fearless? Make sure you join our G.O.L.D. Digga Telegram, Discord, and WhatsApp Group, so that you can get the daily positive quotes we post each day, 365 days of year for inspiration.

"Most people allow their Fear of failure to outweigh their desire to succeed. When you're willing to fail again and again and again, when you make up your mind to become unstoppable, when you make up your mind to become a no matter what person, then that will then give birth to a part of yourself that you don't know right now." – Les Brown

4
Magnetizing Positive Energy

How do you magnetize positive energy you ask? Think of it this way, magnets attract iron due to the influence of the magnetic field upon the iron, according to Google. When exposed to the magnetic field the atoms begin to align their electrons with the flow of the magnetic field, which magnetizes the iron as well. This, in turn, creates an attraction between the two magnetized objects. If that's too technical, to simply put it, you can attract and become a magnet for positive energy by feeling good and being happy.

We all have our own inner thermostatic frequency that enables us to dial into a positive energy or a negative one. The key is to only attract positive energy. In doing so you have to clear your mind, relax, and be open for change. Of course, there will be challenges along the way, but remember, you solve problems. You know what you want, you have mapped it out, and are willing to come up with different resolutions.

Be sure to have a clear vision of what you want to attract into your life first. Everyone goes through life with desires. The desire to want more money, the desire to want a healthy lifestyle, the desire to want great relationships, the desire to want nice belongings, and the desire to want a successful and thriving business. Wouldn't it be great to receive the amount of positive energy it takes to succeed in those that you desire?

If you want to draw positive energy to you like a magnet, you mustn't overthink. When you overthink, it just means, to think about (anything) too much for too long. Stop putting too much emphasis on everything, which way is it supposed to be done, not having everything you think you need, or your personal favorite of all time "I don't have enough time." In doing that, you're bringing that negative vibe to the forefront. I thought you said you wanted to magnetize positive energy.

I haven't spoken about this until now, however, there are two parts to a G.O.AL. Digga. We've already explained the "G.O.A.L." part is an acronym for Generating an Objective Ambitious Lifestyle. That second part is the "Digga." The Digga is just as vital. We dig out those negative influences over our life in order to implement Magnetizing Positive Energy. We can't possibly expect any great outcome with a negative energy level. We insinuate the positive.

It's like this, have you ever woken up out of bed rushing and hit that pinky toe just enough to make you pout? Perhaps the outfit that you want to wear was dirty. Better yet, you're running late for work, you speed to get there only to get a ticket along the way. I say that to say this, it's not always what happens to you, but how you react to it that matters. I'm saying that reminds me of another experience I once had.

I was ready to go on a vacation trip for the weekend for the first time with my adult children and my grandchildren, and the day of departure I suddenly wasn't feeling well. Of course, that didn't stop me, I still made a point to go, and was still excited to go. After all, it had just hit me, and I expected to be better soon. And luckily, for my children and my grandchildren, I had my own room and spent most of my time there.

I was relaxing in the passenger seat the entire drive there to the vacation spot. The atmosphere and accommodations were clean and refreshing. Although I was in bed the entire time with symptoms of a stomach virus, I was content with laying down in peace, while my family enjoyed their outside activities, watching my favorite movies. I still had a sense of happiness despite how I felt. I didn't let not feeling 100% determine the outcome of our trip. I kept the positive energy flowing.

One such inspiring story is that of Lisa Nichols, a successful motivational speaker, author, and entrepreneur. Lisa grew up in difficult circumstances, facing poverty, abuse, and low self-esteem. However, she refused to let her past define her future and instead decided to focus on manifesting positivity in her life.

Through her work as a speaker and coach, Lisa began to teach others how to tap into their own inner strength and create positive change in their lives. She founded her own company, Motivating the Masses, which offers coaching, training, and resources to help people achieve their goals and live their best lives.

One of Lisa's most inspiring achievements was her role in the creation of the movie, *The Secret*, which focused on the law of attraction and the power of positive thinking. Lisa was a featured contributor to the film, sharing her story and offering insights into how to manifest abundance and success.

Through her work and personal journey, Lisa has demonstrated the power of positive energy and the ability to transform one's life through intention and manifestation. She is an inspiration to many, showing that it's possible to rise above difficult circumstances and create a life of purpose and joy.

Magnetizing positive energy is a concept that involves attracting positive energy and transforming it into a powerful force that can be used to enhance our lives. Positive energy is the energy of love, joy, happiness, and peace that we feel within us and around us. It is the energy that motivates us to achieve our goals, inspires us to be kind, and helps us to connect with the world in a positive way.

Magnetizing positive energy is a practice that requires intention, attention, and action. It is not enough to just wish for positive energy to come into our lives; we need to actively seek it out and cultivate it. Here are some tips on how to magnetize positive energy:

Be Grateful: Gratitude is one of the most powerful ways to attract positive energy. When we focus on the things, we are grateful for, we create a positive energy that attracts more positivity into our lives. Make it a habit to write down things you are grateful for every day, even if they are small things like a sunny day or a kind word from a stranger.

Surround Yourself with Positive People: The people we spend time with have a significant impact on our energy levels. Surround yourself with positive people who uplift and inspire you. Spend time with people who make you laugh, who share your interests, and who support your dreams.

Practice Positive Thinking: Our thoughts have a powerful influence on our energy levels. Practice positive thinking by focusing on what is going right in your life, rather than what is going wrong. Replace negative thoughts with positive affirmations and visualize yourself achieving your goals.

Take Care of Your Physical Health: Our physical health is closely linked to our energy levels. I've mentioned this before. Make sure to take care of your body by getting enough sleep, eating nutritious food, and exercising regularly. A healthy body leads to a healthy mind and positive energy.

Practice Meditation: Meditation is a powerful way to calm the mind and connect with positive energy. Practice meditation daily, even if it's just for a few minutes. Focus on your breath and visualize positive energy flowing into your body.

Magnetizing positive energy is a practice that can transform our lives. By cultivating positive energy, we create a powerful force that can help us achieve our goals, connect with others, and find joy and fulfillment in our lives. So, start implementing these tips in your daily life and watch as positive energy flows into your life effortlessly.

Action Steps

It's time, now, to take out that G.O.A.L. Digga Journal of yours and pick up where we left off. Now that you have identified the fear factors and thoughts you have been telling yourself, it's time to become a magnet for positive thoughts. I want you to speak life into your plan. I want you to write down affirmations. Affirmations are the action or process of affirming something.

Start with 5 that you tell yourself each day and add to it each month. Be sure to repeat them to yourself and say them over and over again throughout the day. The purpose of this step is to reprogram your mindset for positive thoughts and to eliminate any fear. Are you ready to become that magnet for positive outcomes?

"If you fight angry, you make a lot of mistakes, and when you fight a sharp witty fighter like me, you can't make mistakes." – Floyd Mayweathe

5

Gratitude and Being Thankful

Always show gratitude, as I mentioned in the previous chapter, and know the importance of being thankful. Gratitude by definition is the quality of being thankful, readiness to show appreciation, and to return kindness. To be thankful is to be pleased and relieved. Without this mindset shift, whatever you consider success to be, your accomplishments will not last long. This is a key skill to magnetizing that positive energy. How can you have positivity without being grateful and thankful? It will be extremely difficult.

The biggest enemies of your success and happiness are negative emotions. Negative emotions can wear you out, they can hold you back, they keep you from being happy. Just think about it: jealousy, rage, self-pity, anger, and depression are all negative emotions. You have to identify the negative emotions and like I stated earlier flip them off like a switch. Replace them with peace, love, joy, and enthusiasm. Chances are that your life will be a whole lot better.

Gratitude is a very powerful emotion that impacts your wellbeing. Taking a few moments out of each day to really appreciate what you have is essential. Gratitude is derived from the Latin word gratia, meaning grace, graciousness, or gratefulness. Gratitude is a highly prized human trait worldwide and one would assume we are morally obligated to feel and express gratitude in response to receiving a benefit. It's more than saying thank you. It's an affirmation of goodness, recognizing that one has obtained a positive outcome and recognizing there is an external source for this positive outcome.

Gratitude is not something that you just have automatically. If you're a person that blames others for your situation or circumstances you find yourself in, then you'll only generate things that make you feel that way. However, if you are a person that has a (how can I get it done mindset), then you will be able to find gratitude and see the positive in every small thing and the good that happens to you will overflow.

Appreciation plays a big role in having gratitude and being thankful. Having appreciation means recognition and enjoyment of the good quality of someone or something. When you develop the capacity to see all good each day, you'll experience several life-enhancing benefits. You have the power to change how you see a rainy day and can turn it into a day full of sunshine and possibilities to be thankful for.

I wake up every morning showing appreciation and gratitude. It's part of my Daily Routine. I have a daily regimen that I practice every day. Part of that is always speaking positivity, not only my affirmations, but also my thoughts of appreciation, showing gratitude, being grateful, and always giving thanks. I have a sign on the wall in my kitchen that I see as I walk past it every day. It states, "Start each day with a grateful heart." That's how I start my day, every day!

As a G.O.A.L. Digga, we have gratitude for the things we receive every day. Whether it be from an outcome we expected or one that was unexpected. We generate grace, we are grateful, we are thankful. Whether we are appreciated or not we express appreciation. We control our emotions.

One remarkable example of gratitude and its transformative power is the life-changing story of John Kralik. John was a struggling attorney who was facing numerous challenges in his personal and professional life. He was overweight, had financial difficulties, and his law practice was on the brink of collapse.

In the midst of despair, John decided to embark on a year-long journey of writing thank you notes. He made a commitment to write one heartfelt thank you note every day for an entire year. His goal was to express gratitude to the people who had made a positive impact on his life, no matter how small.

Initially, John faced skepticism and doubts from those around him, including his friends and colleagues. However, he persisted with his gratitude project, believing that expressing appreciation could bring about positive change.

As John continued to write his thank-you notes, something extraordinary happened. He began to experience a shift in his mindset. He became more aware of the positive aspects of his life, no matter how challenging his circumstances were. This newfound gratitude gave him a renewed sense of purpose and opened his eyes to the opportunities around him.

John's gratitude project had a profound impact on his personal and professional life. He lost weight and improved his health, his relationships became stronger, and his law practice began to thrive. He also discovered that expressing gratitude not only improved his wellbeing but also had a positive impact on the lives of those around him.

Inspired by his transformation, John went on to write a book titled, *365 Thank Yous: The Year a Simple Act of Daily Gratitude Changed My Life*. The book became a bestseller, and John became a sought-after speaker, sharing his story while inspiring others to embrace gratitude in their own lives.

John's story is a powerful reminder of the transformative power of gratitude. By cultivating a grateful mindset and expressing appreciation, we can open doors for growth, attract positive opportunities, and experience a profound shift in our overall wellbeing.

Gratitude is a powerful emotion that has the ability to transform one's life. It is a simple act of being thankful for the good things in life, no matter how small they may be. When we express gratitude, we shift our focus from what we lack to what we have. This simple shift in perspective can have a profound impact on our mental and emotional wellbeing, as well as our relationships with others. Practicing gratitude has been shown to have numerous benefits for our mental and emotional health. Research has shown that people who regularly express gratitude experience higher levels of positive emotions such as happiness, optimism, and contentment. They are also less likely to experience depression, anxiety, and stress.

Expressing gratitude can also improve our physical health. Studies have shown that people who practice gratitude are more likely to engage in healthy behaviors such as exercise, eating well, and getting enough sleep. They also have stronger immune systems and are less likely to experience chronic illnesses such as heart disease and diabetes.

Having gratitude can also improve our relationships with others. When we express gratitude to others, we strengthen our connections with them and build trust. It can also help us to be more empathetic and understanding towards others, which can lead to more fulfilling and satisfying relationships.

There are many ways to practice gratitude, and it's important to find what works best for you. Here are five ideas to get you started:

1. **Keep a gratitude journal:** Each day, I've mentioned this also, write down three things you are grateful for. They can be big or small, but they should be specific.

2. **Express gratitude to others:** Take the time to thank someone who has helped you or made a positive impact in your life.

3. **Practice mindfulness:** Take a few moments each day to focus on the present moment and express gratitude for the good things in your life.

4. **Volunteer:** Helping others can be a great way to express gratitude and make a positive impact in your community.

5. **Take a gratitude walk:** Go for a walk and focus on the beauty around you. Take time to appreciate the simple things in life, such as the sunshine or a beautiful flower.

My point is this, gratitude is an important emotion that can have a positive impact on our mental, emotional, and physical health. It can also improve our relationships with others and help us to lead more fulfilling and satisfying lives. By practicing gratitude regularly, we can shift our focus from what we lack to what we have and appreciate the many blessings in our lives.

Action Steps

In your G.O.A.L. Digga Journal, write down 5 things that you are grateful for. Write down 5 things you are thankful for. I want you to put that up somewhere that you'll see every day. The point of this step would be to remind you to be grateful and thankful and to think about it daily. Are you ready to embrace gratitude?

"Gratitude has the power to mend the mind, heal the heart, and soothe the soul."

– Iyanla Vanzant

6
Sacrifices

Making sacrifices is an integral part of achieving success in any aspect of life. Sacrifices are the choices we make to give up something we value for something else that we believe is more important or necessary. These can range from small sacrifices like giving up a weekend to study for an exam, to big sacrifices like giving up a career to take care of a loved one. The importance of making sacrifices cannot be overstated.

Here are four reasons why:

1. **Achieving goals:** When we make sacrifices, we often do so to achieve a specific goal. Whether it's working extra hours to save money for a down payment on a house or giving up unhealthy habits to improve our health, sacrifices are necessary to reach our goals.

2. **Building character:** Sacrifices require discipline, dedication, and hard work. When we make sacrifices, we learn valuable lessons about perseverance, self-control, and delayed gratification. These experiences help us build character and develop important life skills that can be applied in all areas of our lives.

3. **Prioritizing values:** Making sacrifices forces us to prioritize our values and determine what is truly important to us. This can help us make more informed decisions in the future and lead a more meaningful life.

4. **Fostering relationships:** Sacrifices can also be important in fostering healthy relationships. Sometimes, we need to make sacrifices for the people we care about whether it's giving up our own time to help a friend in need or compromising with a partner to maintain a healthy relationship.

Of course, making sacrifices is not always easy. It can be difficult to give up something we value, especially if it's something we enjoy or are accustomed to. However, it's important to remember that sacrifices are often temporary and can lead to long-term benefits.

It's also important to make sure that the sacrifices we make align with our values and goals. Sacrificing something that is not important to us or that goes against our values will not lead to true success or fulfillment. Making sacrifices is an important part of achieving success and living a meaningful life. By prioritizing our goals, building character, and fostering relationships, we can make sacrifices that lead to positive outcomes and a more fulfilling life.

What is that old saying? "With great power comes great responsibility." Well, it also comes with great sacrifice. When mentioning sacrifice, we don't mean the religious term for slaughter. It's a personal sacrifice and is defined; If you sacrifice something that is valuable or important, you give it up, usually to obtain something else for yourself or for other people.

Speaking of Sacrifice, let's talk about Colin Powell, a retired four-star general in the United States Army and the first Black person to serve as the Secretary of State for the United States.

Powell was born in Harlem, New York in 1937 and grew up in a modest family. He excelled in school and went on to attend the City College of New York (CCNY), where he earned a degree in geology. After college, Powell joined the army and served two tours of duty in Vietnam. He was recognized for his leadership and was eventually promoted to the rank of general. Despite his success in the military, Powell faced racial discrimination throughout his career. However, he refused to let that hold him back. He knew that if he wanted to succeed, he would have to make sacrifices and work twice as hard as his white counterparts.

One of the sacrifices Powell made was moving his family multiple times throughout his career, uprooting his wife and children from their home and friends. He also worked long hours and was often away from his family for extended periods of time. However, Powell's hard work and sacrifices paid off. He became the first Black person to serve as the National Security Advisor, and later the first Black person to serve as the Chair of the Joint Chiefs of Staff. He was also awarded numerous military honors, including the Purple Heart and the Presidential Medal of Freedom.

Powell's story is a testament to the importance of making sacrifices to succeed. Despite facing discrimination and adversity, he refused to give up on his dreams and worked tirelessly to achieve his goals. His story serves as an inspiration to anyone who may be facing obstacles in their life and shows that with hard work, dedication, and sacrifice, anything is possible.

It's not easy when you're making sacrifices. I have struggled for the last 6 years with maintaining my ideal weight. It has been a roller coaster ride. So, I made a goal for myself to keep my weight down. Now, I love to eat, especially chocolate. I love dining out and having a new experience at different restaurants. I especially love a great glass of wine. Who likes to work out? Not me. But I knew I had to do something different, or I would continue to get the same results. So, I made some sacrifices.

I understand there are some sacrifices that I have to make for me to accomplish my goals. So, for me, if I wanted to maintain that ideal weight for myself, I had to give up something. I had to do something different. I stopped using the excuses that I was getting older, and it would be harder. No, I had to sacrifice some things that I was comfortable doing. I didn't have to give up everything, I just made a few adjustments and stuck to it. After all, I had a lot to do with the weight that I had gotten uncomfortable with.

So, remember how I don't like working out? Well, one of the first adjustments that I made for myself, a goal, was to walk more. I started walking 5 times a week at least 4 miles per day. Let me tell you, that was the most comforting, relaxing, and enjoyable time of my day, it was amazing. All I was doing was walking. Don't underestimate a good walk. I lost 20 lbs. with that alone.

I also had to cut back on my alcohol consumption. As I said, I love a good glass of wine. But the way I cut that was to only have one on the weekends or only at social functions. I limit myself to one satisfying full glass of wine. I'm laughing out loud, by the way. I'm not perfect. I slip up from time to time. But you understand what I'm talking about.

Loving to eat is something very addictive. I really had to control this one. I don't eat pork anymore and I cut out red meat. Chicken is still something I crave every now and again, but for the most part, I've almost eliminated it. I don't eat any dairy (I must admit I still eat cheese from time to time though). It didn't sound like much, however, for my body type, it also contributed to an additional 10 lbs. that I lost, without even trying.

If making sacrifices was easy, everyone would be doing it. That's why it's hard for some people to be successful. It takes sacrifice to be successful. No one wants to give up anything they've been doing over and over, the things that they're comfortable with. People usually want to have their cake and eat it too. But it is a give and take situation. You have to give a little to get a little.

As a G.O.A.L. Digga, we do the things that most people won't do, to get the things that most people don't have. We make the necessary sacrifices it takes to get things done. We know how to give things up, but we don't give up. We are creators. When people see nothing there we make something appear.

Action Steps

I want you to take out your G.O.A.L. Digga Journal again. This time I want you to write the things that you're willing to let go of to become the person you want to be. That list may include friends, family, associates, your job, or just bad habits. What are the sacrifices that you need to make in your life? Are you willing to let bad habits go?

"If you want to fly, you got to give up the s*** that weighs you down." – Toni Morrison

7
Waiting on What?

Procrastination is a common human tendency that often holds people back from achieving their goals. Many people tend to put things off until the last minute, thinking that they will have more time to complete their tasks in the future. However, this kind of thinking can be counterproductive, and can actually hinder your ability to achieve your goals. In this chapter, we will discuss the importance of getting started now and not waiting to achieve your goals.

One of the main reasons why you should get started now and not wait to achieve your goals is that time is limited. Every day, we are faced with a finite amount of time, and we cannot get back the time that we have lost. Therefore, it is essential to make the most of the time that we have and to use it wisely. If you wait too long to get started on your goals, you may find that you have run out of time and are unable to achieve what you set out to do.

Another reason why it is important to get started now is that procrastination can lead to a lack of motivation. When we put things off, we are more likely to lose interest in them, and we may start to feel overwhelmed by the amount of work that we have to do. This can lead to a lack of motivation and a feeling of defeat before we even begin. On the other hand, when we start working towards our goals right away, we can build momentum and develop a sense of excitement and enthusiasm that can carry us through to the end.

Additionally, getting started early can give you a head start on the competition. If you have a goal that you want to achieve, chances are that other people have similar goals as well. By getting started early, you can establish yourself as a leader in your field and gain a competitive advantage over others who are waiting to get started.

If you get started now, it can help you to develop a habit of action. When we make a habit of putting things off, we are more likely to continue doing so in the future. On the other hand, when we make a habit of taking action and getting things done, we are more likely to continue doing so in the future. By starting now and developing a habit of action, you can set yourself up for success in all areas of your life.

Tim Urban is a popular blogger and speaker. Tim had always been a procrastinator. He would wait until the last minute to complete tasks, and this habit continued even when he started his blog, "Wait But Why." He would often leave blog posts until the night before they were due, which caused him a lot of stress.

However, Tim realized that his procrastination was holding him back from achieving his goals. He wanted to write more thought-provoking articles and connect with his readers on a deeper level, but he knew that he needed to change his habits to do so.

So, he decided to take action. Tim set a goal to write a post every week, no matter what. He created a strict schedule and stuck to it, forcing himself to write even when he didn't feel like it. He also began to break down his goals into smaller, more manageable tasks, which made them seem less daunting. With this new mindset and approach, Tim was able to produce some of his most insightful and impactful articles. His blog started to gain a massive following, so much so that he was invited to speak at TED Talks.

Today, Tim is an inspiration to many people who struggle with procrastination. He shows that it's possible to overcome this habit and achieve your goals, no matter how big or small they may seem. By taking action and creating a plan, anyone can make progress toward their dreams.

Getting started now and not waiting to achieve your goals is essential if you want to be successful. Time is limited, and procrastination can lead to a lack of motivation, a lack of competitive advantage, and a habit of inaction. By getting started early, you can make the most of your time, develop a habit of action, and set yourself up for success in all areas of your life. So don't wait any longer – start working towards your goals today.

Let's goooooooooooooooo! What are you waiting on? I always ask this to the people I serve. And I have yet to get a reasonable answer. You "Waiting on What"? Even when I get an answer. I still ask, "WHAT ARE YOU WAITING ON"? There's only one answer that I will accept. Which is the only reasonable one, for you to admit that you're waiting on yourself to do something. I only hear excuses, and no reasons. I should know, I used to make those same excuses. When you admit that to yourself, then and only then will you truly begin.

Don't play the blame game. You make the choices that determine your outcome. I've heard it all; This is the way I am. I don't have enough money. I'm waiting until I move into my new place. I'm waiting until I get my taxes. I have to get an iPhone first. I need a better camera. I don't know where to start. I don't have time. I'll do it next year. I need to get a car first. Although these things may be true, these are not reasons to not get started. Don't focus on the past and what you should have done. Take action now.

That's when I pull out that siren in my voice and say. "LET'S GOOOOOOOOOOOOOOOO!" Your decisions brought you to your destination. You know at this point in your life is not where you want to be. You know you're capable of more. You also know you want more. So, when are you going to decide to make different decisions? When are you going to tell yourself that you're ready? When are you going to make that leap?

So many times, you've found yourself looking back at what you could have accomplished by now, if only you had gotten started sooner. You start and quit over and over again. You didn't stay consistent and complete the task. As I mentioned before, we all have made those same New Year's resolutions year after year. So, stop waiting and move into action. Now is the time, and it's as good as any other time to take action.

G.O.A.L Diggas don't procrastinate. We delegate. We make things happen. We find ways to stay motivated. We are doers. We put an action plan together and follow all the steps to the end. We reevaluate when needed and we adjust when necessary. We wait on no one or nothing. We take full responsibility and ownership for our results.

Why wait for tomorrow to do what can be done today? When I say that, I'm asking, when there is something in life that you want to accomplish, why not start now? Get on that path to getting it done. That's the only way you're going to get closer to it, by walking towards it in a sense. Figure out what those steps are and get started. Don't wait, do it now and make that happen. Put one foot in front of the other and GO! There's no need to wait.

If there were a million dollars waiting for you at the end of an obstacle course, would you go through the obstacles to get it? Of course, you would. At least I hope you will. Look at it this way, your success depends on you, and you alone have the ability to go and get it. It's waiting on you. All you have to do is go and get it. I know it doesn't seem that easy, but it is. Think, instead of a million dollars at the end of the road, it's a better you. One who is living out your dreams, whatever that looks like for you.

Action Steps

Let's take out that handy dandy G.O.A.L. Digga Journal. Let's make it really fun this time. Go back to your Aspirational Vision that you completed in Chapter 1. Pick three things off that list that you can turn into goals. Goals you can execute in the next 3 months. Don't worry about the structure right now. We're going to get into how to do that. Write down the things that you can do now to get you closer to accomplishing the goal(s). You're not waiting anymore; you've waited long enough. Are you ready? Let's Go.

"You can't just sit there and wait for people to give you that golden dream. You got to get out there and make it happen for yourself." – Diana Ross

8
Knowing What You Really Want

When it comes to achieving your goals, knowing what you really want is one of the most important factors in determining your success. Far too often, people set goals based on what they think they should want, or what others want for them, rather than what they truly desire. In this chapter, we will explore the importance of knowing what you really want when setting goals.

First and foremost, knowing what you really want helps you to set meaningful and achievable goals. When you set goals that are aligned with your true desires, you are more likely to be motivated and committed to achieving them. You will have a clear vision of what you want to accomplish and why it matters to you, which will help you stay focused and persistent in the face of obstacles.

Secondly, when you know what you want it allows you to prioritize your goals and make the best use of your time and energy. When you have a clear understanding of your priorities, you can focus on the goals that are most important to you and avoid wasting time on tasks that don't align with your values and interests. This will help you to be more efficient and effective in your pursuit of your goals.

In addition, knowing can help you to overcome fear and uncertainty. When you set goals based on what others expect of you, or what you think you should want, you may feel unsure or hesitant about whether you can truly achieve them. However, when you set goals that align with your true desires, you will have a greater sense of purpose and confidence, which can help you to push through fear and uncertainty and stay committed to your goals.

It helps you to create a more fulfilling and satisfying life. When you set goals that align with your values, passions, and interests, you are more likely to experience a sense of purpose and meaning in your life. You will feel more fulfilled and satisfied as you work towards your goals, and you will be more likely to achieve a sense of balance and harmony in your life.

Elon Musk, the renowned entrepreneur, and visionary behind companies such as Tesla, SpaceX, and Neuralink, is a great example. From a young age, Musk knew exactly what he wanted to accomplish in life. He had a clear vision of transforming the world and pushing the boundaries of technology to create a better future for humanity. His ambition was to revolutionize the electric car industry, make space travel more accessible, and advance the field of artificial intelligence.

Instead of settling for a comfortable life, Musk relentlessly pursued his goals. In the late 1990s, he co-founded Zip2, a software company that provided business directories and maps for newspapers. After selling Zip2, he went on to create X.com, which later became PayPal, an online payment system that revolutionized e-commerce.

Despite achieving considerable success with PayPal, Musk was not content. He believed that renewable energy and electric vehicles were the keys to reducing humanity's dependence on fossil fuels and combating climate change. So, he set out to build an electric car company.

With Tesla Motors, Musk faced many challenges, including skepticism from the automotive industry and financial difficulties. However, his unwavering belief in the potential of electric vehicles pushed him to overcome those obstacles. Today, Tesla is one of the most valuable automakers globally, leading the electric vehicle revolution and driving the adoption of sustainable transportation.

Musk's aspirations didn't stop there. He turned his attention to space exploration and founded SpaceX with the mission of making life multi-planetary. SpaceX faced many setbacks and failures along the way, but Musk's determination never wavered. In 2020, SpaceX achieved a historic milestone by successfully launching humans into space and docking with the International Space Station, marking a significant leap forward in commercial space travel.

Musk's commitment to innovation and his relentless pursuit of his goals have made him an inspirational figure for countless individuals. He exemplifies the power of knowing exactly what you want and dedicating your life to its realization. Elon Musk's story serves as a reminder that with passion, determination, and a clear vision, anyone can make a significant impact on the world and accomplish their goals.

To know is essential when setting goals. It allows you to set meaningful and achievable goals, prioritize your time and energy, overcome fear and uncertainty, and create a more fulfilling and satisfying life. So, take the time to reflect on your true desires and values, and set goals that align with them. You'll be amazed at how much easier it is to achieve success when you know what you truly want.

The great billionaire H. L. Hunt was once asked the secret of success. He replied that success only required two things and two things only. First, he said, you must know exactly what it is you want. Most people never make this decision. Second, he said, you must determine the price that you will have to pay to achieve it and then get busy paying that price. As I mentioned earlier, setting goals, working towards them day by day, and ultimately achieving them is the key to happiness in life.

It's possible to pursue and accomplish a goal, only to find out that the dream you had in your heart was something entirely different. Sometimes, the journey to the goal is more enjoyable than actually attaining it. It's okay to realize that you need to adjust your goals. It's okay to do something different. You may realize that it wasn't a restaurant you wanted but managing a company that interests you more.

For example, I told you earlier in the introduction about the beginning of my entrepreneurial journey. Well, in 2010 I started my first business. It was a restaurant. It was called Big Mama's Hot Pot in honor of my late grandmother, whom everyone called Big Momma.

I was so excited I opened it on her birthday. Not really knowing how to run a business at the time, but was determined to make it work, because after all one of my aunts had agreed to come and partner with me and cook the soul food. You see, most of my aunts had the ability to cook really well, and always dreamed of opening their own restaurants one day.

Happy to be the first person in my family to own a restaurant. I had no worries about if I would fail or not, after all how hard would it be to run a restaurant? All I had to do was have great food, which was great because my auntie could cook. We also had Caribbean food, which by the way, the father of my children was the chef and had expertise in that cuisine. There are some things that went wrong in the restaurant that I didn't calculate, which I won't go into detail here, however, the point is, I decided the restaurant business was not for me. I didn't even like it.

It would be seven more years before I ventured out again on that entrepreneurial path, nonetheless, at the time, I didn't know what I wanted, I was going by my family's desires and dreams. I didn't take the time to sit down and evaluate my desires, dreams, aspirations, or goals for that matter. It was a family dream and I wanted to conquer it. I wanted to be the one that did it first. But I wasn't happy with it. It wasn't my dream, it wasn't my goal, it wasn't my desire.

I want all aspiring G.O.A.L. Diggas to dig down deep and discover your true goals to enjoy your maximum happiness from them. My heart was not in the restaurant business. All money ain't good money. There's nothing more satisfying than to be doing what you truly want to do and have fun doing it. There's no better reward than that.

As G.O.A.L. Diggas, we are strategic. We are in tune with what we want, and we go after it. We are leaders. We are the builders of our legacy. We are visionaries. We are clear with our vision and the path that we have to take in order to get there.

Action Steps

I want you to really spend time on this one. I know I mentioned in all the other chapters how important these steps are. But this one is critical, you have to know what you want, what you truly want, in order to plan where you're going. The steps that I want you to take today in this exercise are to figure out what your desire is. Pull out your G.O.A.L. Digga Journal and go back to your action steps in Chapter 1 when you wrote down your Aspirational Vision. Go back and look at the things you wrote down that you wanted to have, do, and be. Lead with that. What do you really want?

"It is so liberating to really know what I want, what truly makes me happy, what I will not tolerate, I have learned that it is no one else's job to take care of me but me."

– Beyoncé Knowles

9

Be Specific

When setting goals, it's important to be specific in order to ensure that you have a clear understanding of what you want to achieve and how you plan to achieve it. Being specific means creating a goal that is well-defined, clear, and measurable. In this chapter, we will discuss the importance of being specific when writing your goals.

Being specific helps you to create a clear and well-defined goal. When you are specific about what you want to achieve, you will have a clear understanding of what you need to do in order to achieve it. This will help you to stay focused and motivated throughout the process and make it easier for you to measure your progress along the way.

When you are specific it helps you to identify the resources and support that you need to achieve your goal. When you are specific about what you want to achieve, you can identify the resources and support that you need in order to achieve it. This might include things like additional training, mentorship, or support from others. When you are specific about your goal, you can identify these needs and take steps to address them.

Michael Jordan widely regarded as one of the greatest basketball players of all time. Jordan's story is a testament to the power of setting specific goals and working tirelessly towards achieving them. From a young age, Jordan knew he wanted to be a professional basketball player. He set his sights on playing for the NBA and worked relentlessly to make it a reality.

In high school, Jordan was cut from the varsity basketball team. This setback only fueled his determination to improve. He worked on his skills, honing his technique, and building his endurance. By his junior year, he had made the varsity team and was quickly recognized as a standout player. Despite his success in high school, Jordan knew that he had a long way to go to achieve his ultimate goal of playing in the NBA. He enrolled at the University of North Carolina, where he played for the Tar Heels and became a star player.

In 1984, Jordan was drafted by the Chicago Bulls, and his professional career took off. He quickly became one of the most dominant players in the league, leading the Bulls to six championships and earning accolades, including five MVP awards. Jordan's success was not simply a result of his talent; it was also due to his relentless work ethic and his commitment to setting specific goals. He would spend countless hours practicing his shots, working on his footwork, and studying the game. He also had a specific vision of the type of player he wanted to be and the legacy he wanted to leave in the sport.

Today, Jordan is considered a basketball legend, and his legacy extends far beyond the court. His story serves as an inspiration to countless individuals, showing that with a clear vision and a relentless work ethic, anything is possible. Michael Jordan's example highlights the importance of setting specific goals and working tirelessly towards achieving them and demonstrates that achieving great things requires both talent and dedication.

Specificity helps you to measure your progress and track your success. When you set a specific goal, you can easily measure your progress and track your success along the way. This can be incredibly motivating and help you to stay focused and committed to achieving your goal. It also helps you to create a sense of accountability. When you set a specific goal, you can hold yourself accountable for achieving it. You will have a clear understanding of what you need to do in order to achieve your goal, and you can hold yourself accountable for taking the necessary steps to make it happen.

Writing your goals is essential if you want to achieve success. It helps you to create a clear and well-defined goal, identify the resources and support that you need, measure your progress, and track your success, and create a sense of accountability. So, take the time to be specific when writing your goals, and you'll be amazed at how much easier it is to achieve success.

Avoid setting vague goals like being a "good" writer. Be specific! Instead, decide that you want to become a best-selling science fiction author. Instead of deciding to make "a lot" of money, commit to a specific salary figure as the goal you pursue. Instead of saying that you want to get married, determine the qualities your ideal mate will have.

Make your goals sharp and clear. When you create a goal try to specify it and in as much detail as possible. You don't achieve your goals because it's not specific enough.

To help you with this, answer these six questions:

1. Who Is involved?

2. What do you want to accomplish?

3. When will you complete it?

4. Where do you want to do it?

5. Which requirements and/or obstacles might get in your way?

6. Why are you doing it?

It's important to be specific so you'll know where to aim. It's sort of like being at a shooting range. You must aim, concentrate, and focus on the target. When aiming for your goals, you must specify your aim. If you don't, you won't hit your target. When you reach each of these milestones, you'll know for certain you reached your goals.

I remember my first big goal. It was to become a homeowner. At the time it was a big goal for me, because I have been homeless several times before this goal I set for myself. I knew who would be involved, me and my partner at the time. I knew what I needed to accomplish, the credit, the income, and the reserves. I will be moving to the area where I wanted my home to be located, and even the obstacles it took to get it, like fixing my credit and coming up with the deposit. I understand my "Why" I do it for my family and my legacy.

When you are clear and specific about your goals you do not have to worry about how and when they will be achieved. You just have to decide clearly what you want. Everything else will move into place and shift around and happen for you. People will show up out of the blue to help you, circumstances will arrive to you, and your goal will move towards you at the right time and place.

Goals give you direction and meaning. Goals give you a purpose in life. As you move towards your goals you will feel energetic and happier. You feel more confident in your abilities. You feel Worthy. Every time you attain the goals that you sought after, you attain more confidence in achieving even bigger goals and going further. You have the ability to achieve almost any goal that you set for yourself. It is your purpose and responsibility to yourself and your legacy, to invest whatever time and effort is required to become absolutely clear about exactly what it is you want, and how you can best achieve it. The greater clarity you have regarding your true goals, the more of your potential you will unleash for the good in your life you deserve.

You want to develop goal setting habits throughout your life. You want to be like a guided missile in the air that has locked on to its target. Moving inherently towards the things that are important to you. The greatest benefit from goal setting is that goals enable you to control the direction of change in your life. It gives you meaning and purpose in everything you do.

A G.O.A.L Digga knows who is involved. We know what we want to accomplish. We know when we will complete it. We know where you want to do it. We obtain the requirements that are needed and plan for any obstacles that may get in the way. We know why we are doing it.

Action Steps

In your G.O.A.L. Digga Journal, imagine that you have a supernatural ability to achieve any goal you could ever set for yourself. What would that be? Be specific with how to attain it. Use the six questions above to help you with this. Remember the sky's the limit, only you see this. What goals would you set for yourself?

"A goal properly set is halfway reached." – Abraham Lincoln

10
Set Measurable Goals

When it comes to setting goals, one of the most important factors in achieving success is setting measurable goals. A measurable goal is one that can be quantified, tracked, and evaluated. In this chapter, we will explore the importance of setting measurable goals and how to do it effectively.

Setting measurable goals helps you to track your progress and stay motivated. When you set a goal that is measurable, you can track your progress and see how far you have come. This can be incredibly motivating, as you can see the progress that you have made and the progress that you still need to make in order to achieve your goal. This can help you to stay focused and committed to achieving your goal.

It helps you to identify areas for improvement. When you set a measurable goal, you can track your progress and identify areas where you may be struggling. This can help you to identify areas for improvement and make adjustments to your plan in order to achieve your goal more effectively.

Also, it helps you to evaluate your success. When you set a measurable goal, you can evaluate your success based on the progress that you have made. This can help you to determine whether you have achieved your goal or whether you need to make additional adjustments to your plan.

Having measurable goals helps you to create a plan for achieving your goal. When you set a measurable goal, you can break it down into smaller, more manageable tasks. This can help you to create a plan for achieving your goal and ensure that you are taking the necessary steps to achieve success.

Michael Phelps, the most decorated Olympian of all time, understood the importance of setting measurable goals to achieve remarkable success in swimming. Phelps began swimming at a young age and quickly showed tremendous talent and potential. He set his sights on becoming an Olympic champion and set specific, measurable goals to help him get there.

Phelps worked with his coach, Bob Bowman, to break down his long-term goals into smaller, measurable milestones. One of the most significant goals was to break the record for the most gold medals won at a single Olympic Games, a feat that had never been accomplished before. In the lead-up to the 2008 Beijing Olympics, Phelps and Bowman set a series of specific and measurable goals, such as improving his stroke technique, reducing his race times, and increasing his endurance and strength.

Phelps trained relentlessly, often spending up to six hours per day in the pool, six days a week. He also worked on his mental toughness, visualization, and goal-setting skills to help him stay focused and motivated. All of his hard work paid off, as Phelps won eight gold medals at the Beijing Olympics, breaking the previous record of seven. His success didn't stop there.

He continued to set measurable goals for himself, such as breaking world records and winning more Olympic medals. Over the course of his career, Phelps won a total of 28 Olympic medals, 23 of them gold, and set multiple world records.

Phelps' story serves as a powerful reminder of the importance of setting specific, measurable goals to achieve remarkable success. By breaking down his long-term goals into smaller, achievable milestones, Phelps was able to track his progress, stay motivated, and continuously improve. His relentless work ethic and dedication to goal setting have made him an inspiration to countless athletes and individuals around the world.

Measurable goal setting is essential if you want to achieve success. It helps you to track your progress and stay motivated, identify areas for improvement, evaluate your success, and create a plan for achieving your goal. So, take the time to set measurable goals and track your progress along the way, and you'll be amazed at how much easier it is to achieve success.

According to Oxford Languages, measure is a noun meaning, a plan of course of action taken to achieve a particular purpose. What do you want to accomplish in the next year? What do you want in the major areas of your life? Including financial, fitness, family, spiritual, personal business, community, and relationships. You have to write these goals down as a list, keep track of them, and make changes as time goes on.

Every year for the past 5 years I've been having vision board parties. This is a good way to start out with your goals and envision what you want to do for the upcoming year. I remember my first vision board; I had one of my daughters draw a house. We put the number of bedrooms and bathrooms we wanted. We made it a two-story house with a chimney. I wish I still had that vision board today, but we're in the house today. Writing things down is very powerful.

Your goal should be measurable in time (how long it would take you to achieve) and in quantity. For example, decide whether you want to quit smoking or cut down on the number of cigarettes. Your brain needs clear instructions to know where to begin. Giving your mind a clear direction keeps you from procrastinating. How are you going to achieve it if you can't measure it?

Tracking the progress of your goal is an important part of keeping you motivated. Have fun with it. Remember to set milestones for yourself so when you achieve them you can celebrate. You should also reevaluate your goals if you did not reach them. It does not mean it can't be done; you may just have to change a few steps. Making adjustments to your goal is part of being an efficient G.O.A.L. Digga.

One of the objectives is to put action into place in order to reap what we sow. We are smart with our goals. We are strategic. We measure our goals. We make our goals attainable. We make sure our goals are relevant. We set a time when we will get it done. We make adjustments when necessary.

Break your big objective down into smaller objectives. When I wanted to maintain a certain weight goal. I didn't just write down that I want to lose 40 lbs. It was not good enough. I had to measure how long it would take for me to reach that goal and how much I would lose at a time. I had to break down the pounds. I went from wanting to lose 40 lbs., to aiming to lose 3 then 5 lbs. each week for 8 weeks.

It's progress that keeps us motivated, so when you don't make your goals measurable, you will lose that ambition and fail. No one wants to make a goal and not succeed at doing it. We want that goal to happen for us. We want to have those things that we strive for. When you measure how long it would take for you to achieve that goal, it becomes reachable because you can see the distance that it takes to get it. Here are five examples of setting measurable goals:

1. **Increase sales by 10% in the next quarter:** This goal is measurable because it has a specific target - a 10% increase in sales - and a specific timeline - the next quarter. Progress can be tracked by monitoring sales figures and comparing them to previous quarters.

2. **Running a 5k in under 30 minutes:** This goal is measurable because it has a specific target - running a 5k in under 30 minutes - and a specific event to work towards. Progress can be tracked by timing each training run and working towards improving speed and endurance.

3. **Save $5,000 by the end of the year:** This goal is measurable because it has a specific target - saving $5,000 - and a specific timeline - the end of the year. Progress can be tracked by monitoring savings account balances and ensuring that the amount saved each month is on track to meet the goal.

4. **Write a 50,000-word novel by the end of the year:** This goal is measurable because it has a specific target - writing a 50,000-word novel - and a specific timeline - the end of the year. Progress can be tracked by monitoring word count and ensuring that the daily or weekly writing goal is being met.

5. **Learn a new language to a conversational level within 6 months:** This goal is measurable because it has a specific target - achieving a conversational level in a new language - and a specific timeline - within 6 months. Progress can be tracked by taking language proficiency tests, tracking the number of new words learned each week, and practicing speaking with a language partner.

Action Steps

It's time for some action. By now, I shouldn't have to remind you to have that G.O.A.L. Digga Journal out and ready for the next steps. Now I want you to measure the time it will take you to reach your 3 goals you wrote down earlier. It cannot be vague like; I'm going to do it in a year's time. I want you to remember to be specific about this time frame. Use the examples to guide you. Are you ready for a change?

"I truly believe that if you put your goals in writing, speak them out loud, and work for them, they will happen." – Ciara

11.
Lifetime Goals

Setting lifetime goals can be a daunting task, but it is also an incredibly important one. By setting goals for the long-term, you can give yourself direction and purpose, and ensure that you are working towards something meaningful and fulfilling. In this chapter, we will explore how to set lifetime goals that will inspire and motivate you for years to come.

Step 1: Reflect on your values and passions:

The first step in setting lifetime goals is to reflect on your values and passions. Think about what is most important to you in life, and what you are truly passionate about. This might involve asking yourself questions like: What kind of impact do I want to make in the world? What are my core beliefs and values? What brings me the most joy and fulfillment? This self-reflection will help you to identify the areas of life that you want to focus on and the goals that will be most meaningful to you.

Step 2: Identify your long-term vision:

Once you have a sense of your values and passions, the next step is to identify your long-term vision. Think about where you want to be in 5, 10, or 20 years, and what you want your life to look like at that point. This vision might involve career goals, personal goals, or a combination of both. Be as specific as possible about what you want to achieve and what kind of life you want to lead.

Step 3: Break down your vision into specific goals:

With your long-term vision in mind, it's time to break it down into specific goals. These goals should be specific, measurable, achievable, relevant, and time-bound (SMART). For example, if your long-term vision is to become a successful entrepreneur, your goals might include things like launching a business within the next year, securing funding within the next 2 years, and achieving a specific revenue target within 5 years. By breaking down your vision into specific goals, you can ensure that you are working towards it in a focused and achievable way.

Step 4: Create a plan of action:

Once you have identified your specific lifetime goals, the next step is to create a plan of action. This plan should include the steps you need to take in order to achieve each of your goals, as well as a timeline for when you want to achieve them. Be realistic about the time and resources that you have available and be prepared to adjust your plan as you go along.

Step 5: Review and adjust regularly:

Again, it's important to review and adjust your lifetime goals regularly. Life is unpredictable, and your goals may need to change over time as your circumstances and priorities shift. By regularly reviewing your goals and progress, you can ensure that you are still working towards something that is meaningful and fulfilling and make adjustments as needed to ensure that you are on track to achieve your long-term vision.

Malala Yousafzai, the youngest Nobel Prize laureate, understood the importance of setting lifetime goals and how it profoundly impacted her life. Born in Pakistan, Malala grew up in a society where girls' education was often marginalized and restricted. However, from a young age, Malala recognized the power of education and set a lifelong goal to advocate for girls' right to education and bring about positive change in her community. Her passion for education and her determination to bring change led her to become an outspoken activist. She started writing a blog for BBC Urdu under a pseudonym, where she shared her experiences of living under the Taliban's rule and her strong belief in the importance of education for girls.

Tragically, at the age of 15, Malala was targeted and shot by the Taliban while returning home from school. This attack only strengthened her resolve to fight for her cause. After surviving the assassination attempt, she continued her advocacy work on a global scale.

Setting her lifetime goal as a guiding principle, Malala co-founded the Malala Fund, an organization focused on advocating for girls' education and empowering young girls worldwide. She became a powerful voice, delivering speeches at the United Nations and other international platforms, and capturing the world's attention with her courage and unwavering commitment.

Malala's efforts garnered worldwide recognition, and in 2014, she became the youngest recipient of the Nobel Peace Prize at the age of 17. This accolade further elevated her platform, enabling her to reach even more people with her message of education and empowerment.

Malala's story highlights the significance of setting lifetime goals. Despite facing adversity and life-threatening challenges, her unwavering commitment to her goal propelled her forward. By setting her sights on advocating for education throughout her lifetime, she not only transformed her own life but also impacted the lives of millions of girls around the world.

Malala's inspiring journey serves as a reminder that setting lifetime goals can be a driving force for achieving meaningful and lasting change. It demonstrates the power of an individual who knows the importance of their goals and dedicates their life to making a difference, leaving a lasting impact on the world.

When setting lifetime goals is an important process that requires reflection, planning, and dedication. By following these steps, you can identify the goals that are most meaningful to you, create a plan of action, and work towards achieving your long-term vision over time. Remember to stay focused, stay motivated, and stay true to yourself, and you will be well on your way to achieving your lifetime goals.

Let me give you an example of myself: One of my lifetime goals is to become a famous best-selling author. In order to turn that dream into reality, I must draw up a plan of action comprised of smaller goals such as:

- Reading the kind of books I wants to write
- Writing a page a day
- Keeping a journal
- Joining a creative writing workshop where I can get feedback on my work
- Doing a course in writing
- Completing a manuscript
- Looking for agents and publishers

Chances are good that you'll have more than one lifetime goal. Apart from your artistic goal, you can look at the other areas of your life (career, financial, education, spiritual, family, and relationships) and create a lifetime goal for each. You may even have several goals within that one category. For now, just choose one goal for each area.

Think about living a bold and exciting life. Your life is full of opportunities. The journey is amazing, the pursuit of happiness. There's no turning back. When you set big and ambitious goals you're not going to do it without failing. You have to learn from that failure. The key is to not give up. When learning to walk you didn't stop when you fell down you got back up.

G.O.A.L. Diggas when we do things we do them big. We think big. We think long term. We walk that walk and talk that talk. We never give up. We do not overthink it. We break big ambitious lifetime goals down into smaller goals. We triumph over restricted aspects.

If you want to accomplish big things you have to want it badly enough. You have to find things that you're passionate about. Find things that are going to challenge you and make Bodacious Goals. Set goals that transcend your lifetime. Go beyond the range or limits of something. Surpass what you can imagine.

Action Steps

Take out your G.O.A.L. Digga Journal and plan your lifetime goals. What lifetime goals will you set for yourself in your career, financially, educational, spiritual, family, and your relationships? As G.O.A.L. Diggas we always give back, so don't forget about your community goals. Are you ready to write your action plan?

"I'd rather regret the risks that didn't work out than the chances I didn't take at all."

– Simone Biles

12

Ensure Your Goals Reflect Your Own Desire

When it comes to setting goals, it's important to ensure that they reflect your own desires and aspirations. This is because goals that are imposed on us by others or society at large can often feel hollow or unfulfilling and may not motivate us to work towards them. In this chapter, we will explore why it's important to set goals that reflect your own desires, and how to ensure that you are setting goals that truly resonate with you.

Why is it important to set goals that reflect your own desires? There are several reasons why it's important to set goals that reflect your own desires:

1. **Increased motivation:** When you set goals that reflect your own desires, you are more likely to be motivated to work towards them. This is because you have a personal stake in achieving these goals, and they are aligned with your values and interests.

2. **Greater satisfaction:** Achieving goals that are meaningful to you can bring a greater sense of satisfaction and fulfillment. When you set goals that reflect your own desires, you are more likely to feel a sense of pride and accomplishment when you achieve them.

3. **Authenticity:** When you set goals that reflect your own desires, you are being true to yourself and living an authentic life. This can lead to greater happiness and wellbeing, as you are living a life that is in alignment with your true self.

How do you ensure that your goals reflect your own desires? To ensure that your goals reflect your own desires, follow these steps:

1. **Reflect on your values and interests:** Take the time to reflect on what is most important to you in life, and what you are truly interested in. Consider your passions, hobbies, and the things that bring you the most joy.

2. **Identify your own goals:** Based on your values and interests, identify the goals that are most meaningful to you. Ask yourself what you want to achieve in your personal and professional life, and what kind of impact you want to make in the world.

3. **Avoid external pressure:** Try to avoid setting goals based on external pressure or expectations. Instead, focus on what is important to you and what you want to achieve.

4. **Be flexible:** It's important to be flexible with your goals, as your desires and circumstances may change over time. Be prepared to adjust your goals as needed to ensure that they continue to reflect your own desires and aspirations.

5. **Review regularly:** Regularly review your goals to ensure that they are still meaningful and relevant to you. If you find that your goals are no longer aligned with your desires, don't be afraid to revise them.

Setting goals that reflect your own desires is essential for achieving long-term satisfaction and fulfillment. By taking the time to reflect on your values and interests, identifying your own goals, and being flexible and authentic, you can ensure that you are setting goals that truly resonate with you and motivate you to achieve them.

J.K. Rowling, the author of the Harry Potter series, ensured that her goals reflected her own desires and passions. Rowling's journey to success was far from easy. She faced numerous setbacks, including the loss of her mother, a divorce, and a battle with depression. However, throughout her struggles, she held on to her love for writing and her desire to share her stories with the world.

As she wrote the first Harry Potter book, Rowling knew that she wanted to write a story that reflected her own passions and interests. She drew on her own experiences of loneliness and isolation and created a world where magic and wonder could exist alongside everyday struggles and challenges. Despite facing numerous rejections from publishers, Rowling persevered, refusing to compromise her vision for the series. She knew that she wanted to write a story that was true to herself and that would resonate with readers of all ages and backgrounds.

Finally, after a long and challenging journey, Rowling's persistence paid off, and the first Harry Potter book was published in 1997. The book was an instant hit, captivating readers around the world with its magic and charm. Rowling went on to write six more Harry Potter books, all of which were equally successful. She also became a philanthropist, using her success to support various charitable causes and advocate for social justice.

Rowling's story serves as a powerful reminder of the importance of ensuring that our goals reflect our own desires and passions. By staying true to herself and her vision, she was able to create a literary phenomenon that has captivated the world for decades. Her story also shows that, with hard work, perseverance, and a commitment to our passions, we can overcome even the most significant obstacles and achieve remarkable success.

If you want your goals to be achievable, let them be your own ideas. Chase the dreams of your heart, rather than the aspirations other people have for your life. Example: if you want to lose weight simply because your partner wants you to (and you're happy with your body), your lack of motivation will snuff out the success you seek. Life is too short. You have to do something that makes you feel alive!

What is mimetic desire? It's imitative. The basis of mimetic desire is that desire is shaped through models of desire. Have you ever relied on other people to model certain desires for us? The danger of finding new models of desires is that there's always another one. We often look to others in order to know what we desire to have. A great example of that is when I shared about my first business being a restaurant. I desired that only because my family had that desire. Having a restaurant was not my desire.

Finding my own desire was one of the best things that happened to me. I'm able to be the person I've always imagined myself to be. I know how to follow my own desires and create my own destiny. When I write my goals down, I write them intentionally now. I write them with a purpose. I have taken control of my life and have gained the confidence that I need to make all of my desires come true.

You have instinctual drives in this universe of abstract desires that you don't have any kind of internal radar for. There's no mechanism to help you choose between these objects of desire. To have an instinctual drive simply means finding what you need to be at your best in any situation, role, or relationship. There are factors, however, such as upbringing, training, or life experience that influence and change people's behavior over time.

Instinct is the reaction or impulse that is innate or a natural inherited trait. The drive is the vigor or strength that causes you to act, strive, work, or try. We typically have two desires: the big ones and the small ones. The big desires, such as wanting to become a lawyer or climbing Mount Everest. The small desires can be here today and gone tomorrow. Such as the latest trends. Desires that change with the season like a new pair of shoes or a brand of technology.

Chasing your own desires and turning those desires into achievable goals is the key to ensure you achieve what you're aiming for. I just explained why you should not live off others' desires. You're destined to fail when you do that. You have to dig deep and bring out those desires that you have within yourself. Only you can envision that for yourself, and you alone have the power to change your circumstances.

G.O.A.L. Diggas we are destined for greatness. We are devoted to our desires. We are the aspiration of other people's desires. We are devoted to our purpose. We have passion. We know our purpose. We also urge other people to find their desires.

Action Steps

In your G.O.A.L. Digga Journal I want you to reflect on your desires. I want you to think back to the things that you've always wanted to do. Things that if you can have, be, or do anything you ever wanted what would that be? Write down your dreams that you wish for. What are some of the things that, if there was nothing in your way that you'd do? Are you ready to dream big?

"I decided long ago never to walk in anyone's shadow; if I fail, if I succeed, at least I'll live as I believe." –
Whitney Houston

13
Keep it Realistic

When it comes to setting goals, it's also important to keep them realistic. While it's great to have big dreams and aspirations, setting unrealistic goals can lead to frustration and disappointment. In this chapter, we will explore why it's important to keep your goals realistic, and how to ensure that your goals are achievable and attainable.

Why is it important to keep your goals realistic? Here are a few reasons why:

1. **Avoid frustration and disappointment:** When you set unrealistic goals, you may find that you are unable to achieve them. This can lead to frustration and disappointment and may even cause you to give up on your goals altogether.

2. **Increase motivation:** On the other hand, setting realistic goals can increase your motivation and confidence. When you set achievable goals, you are more likely to believe that you can achieve them, which can increase your motivation and drive.

3. **Build momentum:** Achieving realistic goals can also help build momentum towards achieving larger, more ambitious goals. When you set and achieve smaller goals, you gain confidence and experience that can help you tackle bigger challenges down the road.

How can you keep your goals realistic? To keep your goals realistic, follow these steps:

- **Be specific:** When setting your goals, be specific about what you want to achieve. Vague or general goals can be difficult to measure and achieve, making them more prone to being unrealistic.

- **Consider your resources:** Take into account the resources you have available to you, such as time, money, and support. Setting goals that require resources you don't have may make them unrealistic.

- **Break down larger goals:** We talked about this in Chapter 11 when setting lifetime goals. If you have a large, ambitious goal, break it down into smaller, more manageable steps. This can make it easier to achieve and help you avoid feeling overwhelmed.

- **Consider your past experiences:** Reflect on your past experiences to determine what goals you have been able to achieve in the past. Use this information to set realistic goals that are similar in nature.

- **Be flexible:** I can never stress this enough, be prepared to adjust your goals if necessary. Life is unpredictable, and circumstances may change, making your goals less attainable. Be flexible and willing to adjust your goals to ensure they remain realistic.

- **Determine if you have the ability or can gain the necessary skills it takes to achieve your goals:** Take into account any limitations you may have to work with that can make the journey longer or again force you to make adjustments along the way. This is a good way to determine whether a goal is realistic or not.

Chris Nikic, who became the first person with Down syndrome to complete a full Ironman triathlon. His journey began when he was 18 years old and weighed 250 pounds. His parents, Nik and Patty Nikic, wanted to help him improve his physical health, so they encouraged him to start exercising. Chris started with basic workouts like push-ups and sit-ups and gradually worked his way up to running and swimming.

In 2020, Chris set his sights on the ultimate challenge: completing an Ironman triathlon, which involves a 2.4-mile swim, a 112-mile bike ride, and a full marathon (26.2 miles) all in a row.

Despite his Down syndrome diagnosis, Chris was determined to achieve his goal. Along with his coach, Dan Grieb, they worked together to set realistic goals and break down the Ironman into manageable parts. They practiced swimming, biking, and running for months leading up to the race, gradually increasing the distances and intensity of each workout.

On November 7, 2020, Chris Nikic made history by becoming the first person with Down syndrome to complete a full Ironman triathlon. He finished the race in 16 hours, 46 minutes, and 9 seconds, well within the official time limit of 17 hours. Chris's achievement inspired people around the world, showing that with dedication, hard work, and realistic goal setting, anyone can achieve their dreams. He proved that even the biggest and most challenging goals can be broken down into achievable steps, and that anyone can accomplish amazing things if they are willing to put in the effort.

I had to make sure that I was making realistic goals when I started my journey. I also have a long-term goal to have a Global G.O.A.L. Digga Community. In order to do that I have to put a strategic plan together. There are different ways to do that. The main thing is I know it is attainable, so I have the ability to do it. I have the necessary skill, which is what you're reading about now. I have to set aside time to do my research on building a community. Factor the pros and cons and adjust it along the way.

There is a difference between realistic goals and unrealistic goals. An unrealistic goal doesn't have a plan. You can't just live off dreams, hopes, and possibilities. A goal that is unrealistic is when it's so big that you can't see the small steps on how you're going to get there. Setting unrealistic goals can have devastating effects. Every time you set an unrealistic goal for yourself, and you don't obtain it, you lose just a little bit of faith and hope in yourself.

For example, you can't set a goal to make a million dollars and you haven't made a hundred thousand dollars yet. Is not that you can't make a million dollars, it's just that you haven't reached the different milestones to reach it yet. Let's shoot for $10,000, then $50,000, and then maybe $200,000. You see the difference?

I know I said to think big, however, you have to take steps to get to that " Big" goal. So, it's not that you're thinking small, it's that you're setting realistic goals to get to that big goal. With every micro win you get a little more confident.

Without a plan, you plan to fail. Have you ever just gotten into your car and said, "I want to go to a place I've never been to before," and just started driving. Absolutely not. You would be a little more specific. Instead, if you want to go to Huntsville, Alabama; you still wouldn't just get in the car and start driving, no, you have to get the directions, make sure you have the gas, and plan for stops along the way. A realistic goal has an executable plan. Goals with a plan are deliverable and have "by when" dates attached to them.

For example, A more realistic goal for obtaining a million dollars can be done in hundreds of different ways. Having a product to sell is one way. You would need to price that product as well. Let's say you have a $100 product. You would have to get 10,000 people to buy your product to make a million dollars. Or what I would suggest is to make a $10,000 product and sell it to 100 people. You can work with the numbers; all you have to do is math. Once you get that down you can be more specific and see how long it will take you to get to a million dollars by knowing how many units you will sell per month.

Now you may say, how am I going to make a product worth $10,000? I guess I'll write another book on that. For now, you can just follow me on my social media platforms, (Nubian Superstars Academy), where I'm always talking about how to have multiple streams of income. I will give you one way though. Be the expert in your field and create a course. You can also offer one-on-one coaching. Okay I gave you two.

I will say this; G.O.A.L. Diggas impact people. Whether it's micro goals or macro goals, we make sure we add value to this world. We produce change and transformation. We plant seeds in the soil. We continue to grow along the way.

Action Steps

I hope you have your G.O.A.L Digga Planner already. We will be transferring the things you wrote in your G.O.A.L. Digga Journal to it soon. Meanwhile, I want you to think of a product you can sell. If you have your own product, great, use it. It doesn't even have to be your own product, you can become an affiliate for someone else's product, like Especially Yours Affiliate Program. I want you to write a plan for how you are going to generate money from the product. This is going to require some work. Are you ready to do your research?

"The way through the challenge is to get still and ask yourself what the next right move is." – Oprah Winfrey

14
Set a Deadline for Your Goals

Setting deadlines for your goals is an essential component of achieving success. A goal without a deadline is just a dream, and without a clear timeline, it can be difficult to stay motivated and focused. In this chapter, we will go over the importance of setting deadlines for your goals and provide some tips on how to set realistic and effective deadlines.

Why is it important to set deadlines for your goals? Setting deadlines for your goals provides several benefits, including:

- **Increased motivation:** Deadlines can provide a sense of urgency that can increase motivation and help you stay focused on achieving your goal.
- **Better time management:** When you have a deadline, you are forced to prioritize your tasks and manage your time more effectively.

- **Clearer focus:** Deadlines can help you stay focused on your goal, avoiding distractions and procrastination.
- **Improved accountability:** Setting a deadline can help you hold yourself accountable for achieving your goal. It can also provide an opportunity to track your progress and adjust your approach if necessary.

To set effective deadlines for your goals, follow these tips:

- **Be specific:** When setting a deadline, be specific about the date and time. Vague deadlines like "sometime this year" can make it difficult to stay motivated and on track.
- **Consider your resources:** Take into account the resources you have available to you, such as time, money, and support. Setting a deadline that requires more resources than you have can make it unrealistic.

- **Break down larger goals:** If you have a large goal, break it down into smaller, more manageable steps and set deadlines for each step. This can make it easier to achieve and help you avoid feeling overwhelmed.

- **Be realistic:** Setting an unrealistic deadline can lead to frustration and disappointment. Be realistic about what you can achieve within the time frame you have set.

- **Review and adjust:** Regularly review your progress towards your goal and adjust your deadline if necessary. Life is unpredictable, and circumstances may change, so be willing to adjust your timeline to ensure it remains achievable.

Sara Blakely, the founder of Spanx, a billion-dollar shapewear company. Sara Blakely had a vision to create comfortable, yet effective undergarments that would help women feel confident and look their best. She believed in her product and was determined to turn her idea into a successful business. However, she knew that merely having an idea was not enough. She understood the significance of setting deadlines to propel her towards her goals.

In the early stages of Spanx, Sara faced numerous challenges and setbacks. She invested her life savings into the business and faced multiple rejections from potential investors and manufacturers. However, she never lost sight of her goals and continued to set deadlines for herself.

Sara set specific milestones and deadlines to keep herself focused and motivated. She created a timeline for product development, marketing strategies, and sales targets. By doing so, she held herself accountable and ensured that she was continually making progress.

One of Sara's most notable deadlines came when she secured a meeting with a representative from the famous department store, Neiman Marcus. She knew that this meeting could be a turning point for her business. She set a deadline to perfect her pitch, design prototypes, and have a sample product ready for the meeting.

With unwavering determination and a clear deadline in mind, Sara worked tirelessly day and night to meet her goals. She even resorted to cutting the feet off her own pantyhose to create a makeshift prototype. Her efforts paid off, she impressed the Neiman Marcus representative with her passion and product innovation and as a result, Spanx was launched in seven Neiman Marcus stores. The success was immediate, and Spanx quickly gained popularity among women for its comfort and body shaping capabilities. Sara's deadline-driven approach had paid off, and her business began to flourish.

Sara Blakely's story is a testament to the power of setting deadlines. By setting specific targets and holding herself accountable, she transformed her idea into a global empire. Her story inspires others to recognize the importance of setting deadlines for your goals, as they can provide the necessary focus, motivation, and sense of urgency needed to achieve success.

Setting deadlines is essential for achieving success. By supplying a sense of urgency, improving time management, focusing your efforts, and holding yourself accountable, deadlines can help you achieve your goals more effectively. When setting deadlines, be specific, consider your resources, break down larger goals, be realistic, and be willing to adjust your timeline if necessary. With these tips, you can set effective deadlines that help you achieve your dreams.

If you've given yourself 10 years to achieve some large goals, divide that time frame into increments to achieve smaller goals that will lead up to your large goal. The next step is to set a 1-year plan, a 6-month plan, and a one-month plan. Decide what you'll achieve in these time frames.

In the example I used in Chapter 11 about me becoming a famous novelist, I set the task it took to complete my manuscript within a reasonable time frame for myself. I gave myself a month to plan out the novel and then a week to write each chapter. When my first manuscript was finished, I gave myself 3 months to revise it (including the time you must leave the work alone so you can return to it with fresh eyes). I started with a publishing company, but if I didn't have one it may have taken me another 3 months to find the right publisher.

G.O.A.L. Diggas know that deadlines must be set for goal achievement. We are laser focused. We strive under pressure. We keep our goals relevant. We work through limitations. Taylor your task for your goals and your time frames around what works for you! This sets you up with a reasonable expectation of the time it will take you to achieve each goal. Adjust your timeline as necessary to move past challenges along the way as you pursue your goal, but always have the big picture, with your ultimate success in mind.

Deadlines are important when trying to achieve a specific result. Deadlines specify the distance or time that is needed to carry out your goals. Deadlines do not only provide perspective on the task at hand and give an indication of how efficient the selected approach is, but it provides you with a clear focus on achieving the goals you want to achieve.

Without deadlines you lose focus and begin to procrastinate. Whether you're procrastinating because of the tedious work it takes to structure the goal, you can become stressed. And you are not pressured enough with a date to complete the task, that you don't have any pressure to achieve a result. Especially in today's world we have so many distractions with social media and the internet that we don't concentrate or lose focus of time.

You want to create the right deadline for your goal. If you have a deadline that is too long or lucid it will allow you to relax too much, that's where procrastination sets in or what I like to call laziness. Whereas a tighter deadline or shorter one will cause high levels of stress resulting in your performance levels. You want to set deadlines that are workable and realistic and don't overwork yourself with unrealistic deadlines.

When setting a deadline, you want to set time pressure deadlines for each individual task but then building contingency for long-term projects. You want to give yourself positive pressure to allow you to work in your best state and performance. You may have setbacks so allow yourself some breathing room. Deadlines are there to give you focus and output without pressuring you into poor results or performances.

You may not always hit your deadlines. Even though this is the worst-case scenario and while structured deadlines will almost always account for various situations occurring, the key is if a deadline is missed for whatever reason, and you have valid reason and justification for such an event occurring, you should not and cannot blame yourself for such situations. Things don't always work out how we plan them. That's when you learn, regroup and restructure.

Action Steps

Find your lifetime goals you wrote in your G.O.A.L. Digga Journal in chapter 11. Pick one of your lifetime goals and break it down into smaller goals. Remember to keep your goals realistic. Next, set deadlines for those goals. Are you ready to put a deadline on your goals??

"A Goal without a timeline is just a dream." –
Unknown

15

Plan Your Daily and Nightly Routine

Let's get into the Importance of a Daily Routine. Having a daily routine is essential for achieving your goals and maintaining a healthy lifestyle. A daily routine can provide structure and stability to your life, making it easier to prioritize your tasks, manage your time, and stay on track. Here are some reasons why having a daily routine is critical:

- **Increased productivity:** A daily routine can help you increase your productivity by providing structure to your day. When you have a plan for what you need to do each day, you are less likely to waste time on unimportant tasks or procrastinate.

- **Improved time management:** A daily routine can help you manage your time more effectively by breaking down your day into manageable tasks. You can prioritize your tasks and ensure that you have enough time to complete each one.

- **Reduced stress:** A daily routine can help you reduce stress by eliminating the uncertainty and unpredictability of your day. When you know what to expect, you are less likely to feel overwhelmed or anxious.

- **Improved sleep:** A daily routine can help you improve your sleep by establishing a consistent sleep schedule. This can help regulate your circadian rhythms and improve the quality of your sleep.

- **Improved physical and mental health:** A daily routine can help you maintain good physical and mental health by ensuring that you have time for exercise, healthy meals, and self-care activities.

Now let's review the Importance of a Nightly Routine. A nightly routine is just as critical as a daily routine when it comes to maintaining a healthy lifestyle. A nightly routine can help you wind down from your day, prepare for the next day, and improve your sleep quality. Here are some reasons why having a nightly routine is critical:

- **Better sleep quality:** A nightly routine can help you improve the quality of your sleep by signaling to your body that it's time to wind down. This can help you fall asleep faster and stay asleep longer.

- **Reduced stress:** A nightly routine can help you reduce stress by providing a sense of closure to your day. When you have a routine for winding down, you can let go of the stress and anxiety of your day and focus on relaxation.

- **Improved mood:** A nightly routine can help you improve your mood by providing time for self-care activities, such as reading, meditating, or taking a warm bath. These activities can help you relax and improve your mental state.

- **Improved productivity:** A nightly routine can help you improve your productivity by preparing for the next day. You can review your schedule, set goals for the next day, and prepare your workspace. This can help you start your day with a clear plan and focus.

- **Improved physical health:** A nightly routine can help you improve your physical health by establishing a consistent sleep schedule, preparing healthy meals and snacks for the next day, and engaging in self-care activities that promote physical wellbeing.

Having a daily and nightly routine is critical for maintaining a healthy lifestyle, managing your time effectively, and achieving your goals. A daily routine can help you increase productivity, improve time management, reduce stress, and improve physical and mental health. A nightly routine can help you improve sleep quality, reduce stress, improve mood, improve productivity, and improve physical health. By establishing a daily and nightly routine, you can take control of your life and achieve your goals.

Michelle Obama, former First Lady of the United States. Michelle Obama is known for her intelligence, grace, and unwavering dedication to her work. Throughout her time as First Lady, she became a role model for many women around the world, inspiring them to pursue their dreams with determination and hard work. One of the keys to her success was her commitment to maintaining a daily and nightly routine.

Michelle Obama's routine included waking up early in the morning and starting her day with exercise, usually a combination of cardio and strength training. She believed that taking care of her physical health was essential to maintaining her mental and emotional wellbeing, and that exercise gave her the energy and focus she needed to tackle her busy schedule.

After her workout, Michelle would have breakfast with her family and then start her workday. She would spend several hours each day at the White House, attending meetings, giving speeches, and working on various initiatives to support education, health, and other social causes.

In the evenings, Michelle made sure to spend quality time with her family, often having dinner together and reading with her daughters before bed. She also took time for self-care, such as reading, meditating, or spending time in nature.

Michelle's commitment to her daily and nightly routine allowed her to balance her responsibilities as First Lady while maintaining her physical and mental health. She recognized the importance of setting aside time for self-care and taking care of her own needs, as this allowed her to be more present and effective in her work.

Michelle Obama's story is a powerful reminder of the importance of having a daily and nightly routine to achieve one's goals. By prioritizing physical and mental health, setting aside time for family and self-care, and maintaining a disciplined schedule, Michelle was able to accomplish incredible things and inspire others to do the same.

When wanting to create habits for yourself you have to put daily and nightly routines in place. Think of six habits you want to implement in your life, and I want you to do three or four of them each day. It could be going for a walk, meditating, reading, or even writing in your G.O.A.L. Digga Journal. List those habits out on your calendar and every day I want you to do at least four but as many as five. If you only get one done in a day, don't turn around and carry over and do eight the next day to make up for it. Just start over again.

There's a thing called the Dopamine System. Dopamine is a neurotransmitter made in your brain. It plays a role as a "reward center" and in many body functions, including memory, movement, motivation, mood, attention, and more. As a hormone, dopamine is released into your bloodstream. It also plays a small role in the "fight-or-flight" syndrome: the fight or flight response refers to your body's responses to a perceived or real stressful situation, such as needing to escape danger.

Neurons that release dopamine are activated when we expect to receive a reward. That's what I want you to focus on right now. The way a rewards schedule works, is you want to train up a circuitry for giving yourself random intermittent rewards for performing these habits on a regular basis. You want to teach the circuitry to work regularly, be rewarded every once in a while, and at random. So, make it an activity that becomes a habit and reward yourself.

You'll be wise to put certain habits at the earliest part of the day and other habits at the latter part of the day. Like working out, it may be smarter to get it done in the early morning after waking up because your energy levels tend to be higher. Whereas, reading, you may put that on your schedule at the latter part of the day closer to the time for you to go to bed. You basically want to put the things you need to do into the part of the day that will be easiest for you to do.

Surely you have routines already that you don't even think about. You wake up, you brush your teeth, you get dressed, you take your children to school, you go to work, you come home, you cook dinner, you take a shower, and go to bed. I know it's a lot more in between but you get the gist of it. All you have to do now is implement new habits that are going to improve your life and stick with it.

Think of it like this, if you don't do this every day, what ways would the outcome be different from if you did do it every day; what will be your result? Knowing that you are in control of your own reality should be more than enough to motivate you. Be sure to celebrate random intermittent wins. Keep in mind the 85/15 Rule. 85% of the time you're performing correctly, the other 15% of the time you're performing incorrectly.

Decide on the things you'll do each day to achieve your smaller goals. Perhaps if you were to become a novelist, you would write a page every day. You also may want to write in your journal every week. If you stick to your routine, you'll remain motivated.

Once you've divided your lifetime goals into smaller ones, you may find yourself feeling overwhelmed, but all you have to do is prioritize your intermediate goals and keep them practical and achievable. Writing down your goals helps clarify them and also reminds you of them when life is trying to distract you.

Action Steps

I want you to take out your G.O.A.L. Digga Planner this time. In it you will see pages for daily routines and pages for nightly routines. I want you to plan the new habits you want to implement into your life. Write down your daily and nightly routine. It may change from time to time, that's why I've added several copies throughout the planner. Are you ready for New Habits?

"You'll never change your life until you change something you do daily. The secret of your success is found in your daily routine." – Quotebanger

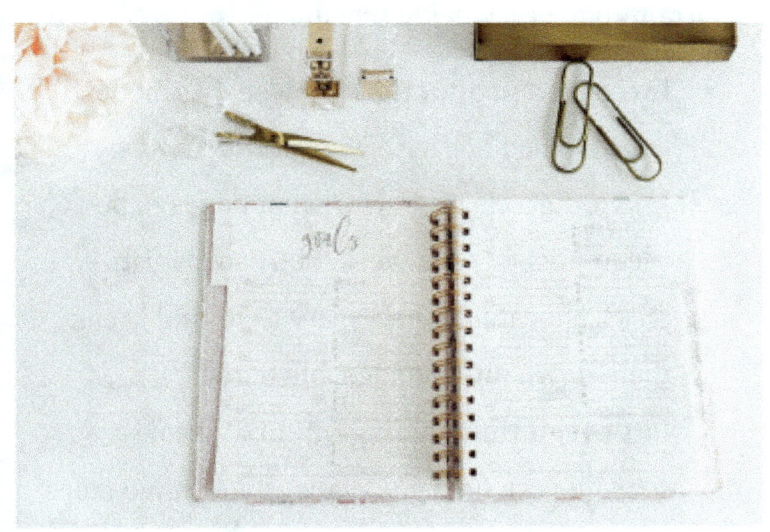

16
Plan Your Weekly Routine

Having a weekly schedule is an essential part of staying organized and on track with your goals. A weekly schedule provides structure and helps you prioritize tasks, allowing you to manage your time more effectively. Here are some reasons why it's important to have a weekly schedule:

- **Increased productivity:** A weekly schedule can help you increase your productivity by providing a clear plan for what needs to be accomplished each week. You can prioritize tasks, allocate the necessary time, and break them down into manageable parts.

- **Improved time management:** A weekly schedule can help you manage your time more effectively by allocating specific times for certain tasks. This can help prevent procrastination and ensure that you have enough time to complete everything on your to-do list.

- **Reduced stress:** A weekly schedule can help you reduce stress by providing a sense of control and organization to your week. When you have a plan in place, you are less likely to feel overwhelmed or anxious about what needs to be done.

- **Improved work-life balance:** A weekly schedule can help you improve your work-life balance by allocating specific times for work, family, and personal time. This can help you avoid burnout and ensure that you have time for the important people and activities in your life.

- **Better goal achievement:** A weekly schedule can help you stay on track with your goals by breaking them down into smaller, achievable steps. You can allocate specific times for working towards your goals and track your progress each week.

- **Improved communication:** A weekly schedule can help improve communication with colleagues, family, and friends by providing a clear understanding of when you are available and when you are not.

- **Improved flexibility:** A weekly schedule can provide the flexibility to adjust your plans as needed, whether due to unforeseen events or changing priorities.

Having a weekly schedule is critical for managing your time effectively, reducing stress, improving work-life balance, achieving your goals, and improving communication. By creating a weekly schedule, you can take control of your week and ensure that you are spending your time on the things that matter most to you.

John H. Johnson, the founder of Ebony and Jet magazines. John H. Johnson was born in Arkansas in 1918 and grew up in poverty during the Jim Crow era. Despite the obstacles he faced, he was determined to succeed and create a better life for himself and his family. He believed that having a structured routine was essential to achieving his goals, and he developed a weekly routine that he followed rigorously throughout his life.

Johnson's weekly routine involved setting aside specific times for work, family, and self-care. He would wake up early in the morning and spend several hours at his desk, working on his magazines and other business ventures. He was a firm believer in the power of hard work and discipline, and he often worked long hours to ensure the success of his publications.

In addition to his work, Johnson was committed to spending time with his family. He would make sure to have dinner with them every evening and would often take his children on trips or outings over the weekends. He believed that family was a crucial part of his life, and he wanted to make sure that he was always present and available for his loved ones.

Finally, Johnson recognized the importance of taking care of his own physical and mental health. He would set aside time each week for exercise, meditation, or other forms of self-care. He believed that taking care of himself was essential to his success in business and his personal life.

Through his disciplined weekly routine, Johnson was able to achieve incredible success as an entrepreneur and pioneer in the media industry. His magazines, Ebony and Jet, became hugely popular and influential publications that celebrated black culture and paved the way for other black-owned media companies.

John H. Johnson's story is a powerful example of how a structured weekly routine can help individuals achieve their goals and dreams. By setting aside time for work, family, and self-care, Johnson was able to balance his responsibilities and accomplish incredible things. His story serves as an inspiration to all, particularly Black men and boys who may face systemic barriers to success.

People sometimes have a misconception of a weekly routine schedule. You may see it as a burden to do things you've put off from doing, because it's unpleasant. So, you avoid it and put it off. Use a schedule to design the days that you would like to have if you were taking care of yourself. You want to set aside time to do this.

So, while you're scheduling your daily and nightly routines, schedule a day to take care of this task. You want to give yourself a couple of hours to get this done. You want to do it before the week that you're scheduling takes place, like on a Friday or even that Sunday before. That way when your week starts you're ready.

Write down everything that you want to accomplish for that week. Now you may have a very long list so make sure you choose 3 big goals and 3 smaller goals. Remember these are tasks that will be completed during that week. Don't get burnt out by trying to add everything that you wrote on that list, there will be other weeks. Consider each task individually, by figuring out which one is important or vital to have.

A good way to make sure you get around to completing your goals for the week is to set up a time block. Remember G.O.A.L. Diggas are executors. I want you to set aside an amount of time to work on your goal. Time blocking helps with that. It's better than a to-do list. Instead of having 1. Write my book, 2. Read, 3. Work out. When blocking the things that I need to get done, you'll schedule a time block, 1:00 to 2:00 write my book, 5:00 to 6:00 read, 8:00 to 9:00 work out, and so forth. This way you only have a certain amount of time to work on your goal with your full attention and enough pressure that you need to finish it.

Before you begin each day, reflect on the goals you have set for yourself. Take about 10 to 15 minutes to go over the task for the day. You can do this during your morning cup of tea or breakfast. Just taking those few moments to reflect will set your day up for massive success. Your morning reflection is the time to go over the things that you have to do throughout the day and remember why you're doing each of them. It gets your day started with a great attitude.

You should also like to complete a nightly reflection as well; it keeps you motivated to see what you've accomplished that day. This will help you unwind your mind. During your nightly reflection you want to remember your why. Why are you doing this? This will help you focus and clarify your priorities so you can plan accordingly. This also gives you a chance to mark off your completed goals and to reschedule the ones that are not completed. Sit back and appreciate your progress. The goals that you have accomplished are done, so give yourself a hand.

In chapter 15 we talked about dopamine and its effect. Our brains love dopamine. Every time you laugh at a video or think something is interesting, our brains get a tiny dose of dopamine. That's why it's so important to celebrate every time you complete a goal. When you cross a goal off of your list jump up and dance, smile, and shout. When completing an even larger goal that took longer, call up a friend and go out for drinks. Whatever you do, make sure you celebrate your wins.

Action Steps

Now I want you to go to your time blocking pages in your G.O.A.L. Digga Planner. The goals that you have chosen for yourself to complete, put them in time blocks. Don't make it too complicated. Just figure out a system that works for you. As each week goes by, try something different. Take the tips that interest you, test them out, and see how it fits into your system. Are you getting it now?

"Don't think about what can happen in a month, don't think about what can happen in a year, just focus on the 24 hours ahead of you and do what you can to get closer to where you want to be." – Unknown

17

The Adventure and Joy of Goal Setting

Goal setting is an adventure that brings joy and excitement to your life. It allows you to explore your desires, aspirations, and dreams, and gives you a roadmap to achieving them. Here are some reasons why goal setting is an adventure that brings joy:

- **It ignites passion:** When you set goals, you are fueling your passion and igniting a fire within you. Goals give you something to strive for, and they help you stay motivated and focused on the things that matter most to you.

- **It creates purpose:** Setting goals creates a sense of purpose in your life. It helps you identify what you want to achieve and gives you direction and meaning.

- **It fosters growth:** Setting and achieving goals requires you to grow and develop in new ways. It challenges you to step out of your comfort zone and take risks, which can lead to personal growth and self-discovery.
- **It brings a sense of accomplishment:** Setting and achieving goals brings a sense of accomplishment and satisfaction. When you reach a goal, you feel proud of yourself and your efforts, which can boost your self-esteem and confidence.
- **It creates memories:** The journey towards achieving your goals creates memories that you can look back on and cherish. The challenges you face and the obstacles you overcome all contribute to the story of your life and make it richer and more meaningful.
- **It brings joy and happiness:** Pursuing your goals brings joy and happiness to your life. It gives you something to look forward to and keeps you motivated to keep moving forward.

Goal setting is an adventure that brings joy and excitement to your life. It ignites your passion, creates purpose, fosters growth, brings a sense of accomplishment, creates memories, and brings joy and happiness. By setting goals and embarking on the journey towards achieving them, you are taking control of your life and creating a life that is meaningful and fulfilling. So, go ahead and set some goals for yourself, and enjoy the adventure!

Maya Angelou, a renowned author, poet, and civil rights activist. Maya Angelou was born in 1928 in St. Louis, Missouri, and faced numerous challenges throughout her life, including poverty, racism, and sexual assault. Despite these obstacles, Angelou was determined to succeed and pursue her passions. One of her greatest passions was writing, and she set numerous goals for herself in this field. She became the first Black woman to write a screenplay that was produced, and she also wrote several books, including the critically acclaimed memoir "I Know Why the Caged Bird Sings."

Angelou's love of writing brought her a great deal of joy and fulfillment, but she also used her talent to advocate for social justice and equality. She was a vocal supporter of the Civil Rights Movement and used her poetry and prose to speak out against racism and discrimination. She was also an accomplished dancer, singer, and actor, and she set goals for herself in these areas as well. She performed on Broadway and toured the world as a singer, using her talents to inspire and uplift others. Despite her success, Angelou never stopped setting new goals for herself. She continued to write and publish books well into her eighties, and she remained active in social justice and activism until her death in 2014.

Maya Angelou's story is a powerful example of the adventure and joy of goal setting. She faced numerous challenges throughout her life but never lost sight of her dreams and passions. Her love of writing, performance, and social justice brought her a great deal of joy and fulfillment, and she continues to inspire others to pursue their own goals with determination and perseverance.

Your life will be much more exciting once you set your goals. Again, every little goal reached will boost your self-confidence and your enjoyment of life. It will also eliminate any fear you may have of failure. You'll banish boredom because there's always something to do and a pot of gold to look forward to at the end of the rainbow. Life is an adventure! What a joy to know that you are in control of your own destiny.

Start planning your life. The time is now! You can be whoever you want. You can go wherever you want. You can have whatever you desire. Your job is to become more valuable. We often set goals that we give up on and never finish. Then we get upset or depressed because we didn't put enough effort into accomplishing it. Sometimes we set a goal without thinking it through, we just set it. To achieve a goal, you have to understand what motivates you to persevere in it.

Think of the areas in your life that you want to enhance and ask yourself these two questions: How do you want to feel? What would give you that feeling? This is a different approach to how to write a goal. You want to get to the heart of what you really want when you set a goal. Whether it's a career change you want to have, the money you'd like to have, or the relationship you want. Each one ultimately is going to produce a feeling that you want to have. So set the goals that will give you that feeling that you want.

For example: If you want to feel inspired, loved, and free to love. The desire for these feelings will lead you to goals that allow you to have those feelings like a high-rise condo, or an emotionally available relationship. So, it starts with how you want to feel and what will give you that feeling. Look at it as setting up systems instead of making goals. You are putting a system in place in order to accomplish your goals. You don't want to set a goal unless you have a system around it. If you have the right system in place you can achieve any goal set. Let's break it down into five different steps.

Step One: Write down the goal. You have to know where you're going in order to get there. People can tell you how to set up your browser to optimize your tab, however, what's the point in that if you cannot drive customers to your website? What's the point of being productive if you don't know where you're going. The key to having a goal is something you currently don't have which will make you do something that you currently aren't doing.

Step Two: Have a strategy. Think of what has worked for you in the past and also think of what has worked for others. What are some of the things that you have done that have given you big results versus smaller results? Is there anyone in your industry that has succeeded despite their obstacles? What did they do differently? So, take what has worked for you and worked for others and come up with your strategy.

Step Three: Do the one-time actions first. These are the actions that you do only one time and you reap the benefits for life. What can you eliminate? Where can you find an expert to complete this task? How can you change your environment? What influencers should you hang around? A lot of times it just takes getting an expert opinion on how to do something. You can do this by joining our G.O.A.L. Diggas community across our social media platforms, or a coaching call by yours truly, just go to my Instagram page and book a free 15-minute consultation. You can also email me at info@goaldigga.org. Experts will give you the feedback to move you forward.

Step Four: Have a system for daily and weekly actions steps. You have something to do every day and every week to move you forward to that goal. I have created the tools that you need to accomplish this. You have access to the G.O.A.L. Digga Journal and the Planner. If not, go to my website www.goaldigga.org and get yours now!

Step Five: Take action and stay committed. A plan is just a wish without action. I want you to use what I like to call the 10/30/90 Day Rule. So, for 10 days test your goal out to see if it is sustainable. If you can do it for 10 days you probably can do it longer. If not, you may have to regroup and try something new. If it is something you can do, move forward to 30 days, you want to work on getting to see some progress. If you can do it for 30 days you can do it for 90 and then you'll see the results. Even if you accomplish 80% using this rule you'll still be successful.

Action Steps

I want you to take a moment to reflect on everything you are learning in this book. Write down in your G.O.A.L. Digga Journal your takeaways thus far. What have you implemented so far? Have you had to revise your goals? You have really come a long way. I hope that you have been keeping great notes in your G.O.A.L. Digga Journal. You are getting closer and closer to becoming an efficient G.O.A.L. Digga. Aren't you excited?

"Embrace what makes you unique, even if it makes other people uncomfortable. I didn't have to become perfect because I learned throughout my journey that perfection is the enemy of greatness"

– Janelle Monroe

18
Help with Setting Goals

Setting goals can be a challenging process, but you don't have to do it alone. There are many resources available to help you achieve your goals. Here are some ways to get help when setting goals:

- **Seek out a mentor:** A mentor can provide guidance and support as you set and work towards your goals. They can share their own experiences and provide insight into the challenges you may face. Remember you can book a free 15-minute consultation call with me by also going to my website www.goaldigga.org.

- **Join a support group:** Joining a support group can provide you with a community of like-minded individuals who are also working towards their goals. You can share your progress, discuss challenges, and gain motivation from others. Don't forget to join the G.O.A.L. Digga Community by following our social media platforms and joining our

WhatsApp, Telegram, and Discord Groups.

- **Hire a coach:** A coach can help you set and achieve your goals by providing accountability, support, and guidance. They can help you identify your strengths and weaknesses, create an action plan, and track your progress. I'm your Accountability Coach! Look out for my future webinars where I go in depth in structuring your goals.
- **Use online resources:** There are many online resources available to help you set and achieve your goals. You can find blogs, podcasts, and courses that provide tips and strategies for goal setting and achievement. I also have a separate social media platform that you're welcome to join, catering to Inspiring Entrepreneurs called Nubian Superstars Academy as I mentioned in the beginning of the book.

- **Read books:** There are many books on goal setting and achievement that can provide inspiration and guidance. You can find books on specific topics, such as productivity, time management, or self-improvement. I also want to point out the power of audio books. You can listen to books while traveling, exercising, or waiting at the doctor's office.

- **Ask for help from family and friends:** Your family and friends can provide support and encouragement as you work towards your goals. They can help you stay accountable and provide a listening ear when you need it. Now, I only say this if they are in support of what you do. Not everybody is going to see your mission or understand your goals. Keep that in mind.

John Thompson, a legendary basketball coach, who became the first Black head coach to win an NCAA championship. John Thompson was born in 1941 in Washington, D.C., and faced numerous challenges growing up, including poverty and racism. Despite these obstacles, he excelled in basketball and was recruited to play for Providence College. After his playing career ended, Thompson went on to become a successful coach, eventually landing the head coaching job at Georgetown University in 1972.

At Georgetown, Thompson faced numerous challenges, including a lack of resources and a history of racism in the basketball program. But he was determined to build a winning team and create opportunities for his players, many of whom came from disadvantaged backgrounds. One of the keys to Thompson's success was his ability to set goals and enlist the help of others in achieving them. He worked closely with his assistant coaches and support staff to create a team culture of hard work, discipline, and accountability. He also emphasized the importance of academic achievement and encouraged his players to set goals in their studies as well as in basketball.

Under Thompson's leadership, the Georgetown basketball program flourished. The team made it to the NCAA championship game three times, winning the title in 1984. Thompson became a beloved figure in the basketball world, known for his dedication to his players and his commitment to social justice.

Thompson's story is an inspiring example of the importance of having help with setting goals. He recognized that achieving his goals would require the support and collaboration of others, and he worked tirelessly to create a team culture of shared goals and values. His success as a coach and leader continues to inspire others to pursue their own goals with the help of a supportive community.

Setting and achieving goals can be a challenging process, but you don't have to do it alone. There are many resources available to help you along the way, including mentors, support groups, coaches, online resources, books, and family and friends. By seeking out help when you need it, you can increase your chances of success and achieve your goals more efficiently.

So, don't be afraid to ask for help, and remember that there are people and resources available to support you on your journey towards achieving your goals. The following questions will help you begin the process of goal setting. Answer them honestly.

- What was your life like 5 years ago? What job did you have? Were you in a relationship? How much did you weigh? These types of historical things.
- Where was your family life 5 years ago? Where were you spiritually? Where were you in your career, or in your business? Where were you financially? What did it look like? What was your attitude like? What was your mindset like? Overall, you just want to assess how you were 5 years ago.
- Where are you today? Ask yourself those same questions from 5 years ago and reflect on today. How far have you come? Where do you want to go? You want to get an idea of how much growth you've had. You want to also recognize where you have been falling short. Where have you not put your focus and concentration on?

- How many books have you read in the last 5 years? Who's been coaching you? How many conferences have you gone to? What have you done far as self-development? What have you learned in those different areas?

- How balanced is your life? Do you constantly encounter extremes in circumstances? For instance you might feel too rushed or too stressed out to spend enough time on the things that are important and worthwhile. How can you balance your life and schedule time each day to work towards your goal(s)?

- Do you have a sense of purpose? What are your most important core values? What matters most to you? What goals can you set that support this purpose?

- Are your thoughts and behavior patterns getting in the way of a happy, successful life? Are you habitually pessimistic? Are your feelings of success dependent on what others think of you? How can you banish these limiting beliefs?

- What are your main goals? You can brainstorm this; nothing is set in stone. Is it something you really want to do? How important is it to you? You want to limit yourself to three to six main goals.
- Why do you want to achieve that goal? How does that goal relate to you living your dream life? Every goal that you set for yourself should get you closer to the life that you want to create.
- Where do you want to be 5 years from today? Remember the adventure part in chapter 18, your goals will take you as far as your mind will let you.

Once you have some answers, you can ask yourself which of these areas are the most important for you to work on. Jot down the benefits of the goal(s) you set and the challenges you're likely to face on your journey of self-development. Whatever you track and measure improves. It also accelerates when we report it to others. Pursue what you're passionate about that will make you happiest.

Action Steps

In the front of your G.O.A.L. Digga Planner you should see an area to write down your big bodacious goals for each area of your life. I want you to write down three measurable "Goals" in each area that you want to produce over the next 5 years. When you have a business it's important to write a business plan. Your life is important, so you have to write a Life Plan.

"Work like hell. Put in 100-hour weeks every week. if others are putting in 40 hours and you're putting in 100, even if you're doing the same thing you will achieve in 4 months what it takes them a year." - Elon Musk

19
Welcome Change

Change is an inevitable part of life, embracing change can be a powerful tool in goal setting. Here are some reasons why welcoming change can be beneficial in achieving your goals:

- **Opens up new opportunities:** Embracing change can open up new opportunities and possibilities that you may not have considered before. Being open to new ideas and approaches can lead to innovative solutions and breakthroughs in achieving your goals.

- **Increases resilience:** Embracing change can increase your resilience and adaptability in the face of challenges. It allows you to be flexible and adjust your goals and plans, when necessary, rather than giving up in the face of adversity.

- **Encourages growth:** Embracing change can encourage personal and professional growth. It allows you to learn from your experiences and develop new skills and knowledge that can help you achieve your goals.

- **Sparks creativity:** Embracing change can spark creativity and inspire new ideas. It can lead to a fresh perspective on your goals and how to achieve them.

- **Fosters a positive mindset:** Embracing change can help you develop a positive mindset. Rather than fearing change, you can view it as an opportunity for growth and progress.

- **Keeps you motivated:** Embracing change can keep you motivated and engaged in the pursuit of your goals. It can bring excitement and energy to the process, keeping you focused and inspired.

Welcoming change in your goal setting can be a powerful tool for achieving success. It opens up new opportunities, increases resilience, encourages growth, sparks creativity, fosters a positive mindset, and keeps you motivated. By embracing change and being open to new ideas and approaches, you can stay on track towards achieving your goals, even in the face of challenges and obstacles. So, don't be afraid of change – embrace it, and see how it can help you achieve your goals and live a fulfilling life.

Jeff Bezos, the founder of Amazon. Bezos founded Amazon in 1994 as an online bookstore, but he quickly realized that the company had the potential to become much more than that. He expanded Amazon's product offerings to include a wide range of goods and services, and the company quickly became one of the world's largest retailers.

But Bezos did not stop there. He recognized the importance of staying ahead of the curve and embracing change in order to stay relevant and continue growing. In 2007, he introduced the Kindle, a revolutionary e-reader that allowed customers to download and read books on a portable device. The Kindle became an instant success, and it helped cement Amazon's position as a leader in the tech industry.

Bezos has continued to embrace change throughout his career, constantly looking for new ways to innovate and improve. In recent years, he has shifted his focus to space exploration, founding the company Blue Origin and investing billions of dollars in developing new technologies for space travel.

Bezos' story is an inspiring example of the importance of welcoming change when setting goals. He recognized that success is not a static state, but rather an ongoing process of adaptation and growth. By constantly looking for new opportunities and embracing new technologies, Bezos was able to build one of the world's most successful companies and continue to push the boundaries of what is possible. His example serves as a reminder that change is not something to be feared or resisted, but rather a necessary and exciting part of achieving our goals.

Be prepared to flow with the changes in your life. This way, you'll be in sync with the universal flow and life will run more smoothly. The only constant in life is change. You may not like change but what's the alternative? Every single day you have a chance to make a choice. You are able to move yourself into that direction that you desire and deserve.

As you grow older, your priorities may change. What you wanted to achieve years ago may be less important today. So, it's a good idea to review your goals from time to time. Choose the goals that are most important to you now. Put yourself in control of the changes ahead. You have that ability.

There are only a few pinpoint choices that can be made to change your life. You can choose to do less of something. You can choose to stop doing something. You can choose to do more of something. Or you can choose to start doing something. These are the decisions that you will have to make in order to get a different result in your life.

What do you want to cut back on? There may be some things in your life that you want to do less of. You might be spending too much time on social media for entertainment purposes. So, you may want to go from 3 hours a day to one hour a day. You may want to show less emotion when dealing with conflict. So, you may want to count down from 20 before responding to confrontation. When you choose better you do better.

What do you want to completely stop doing? You want to stop doing things that's harming you or keeping you from getting the things you want. You may want to stop making excuses or stop complaining about your circumstances. If you don't do anything you won't get anything. You must do the work. Maybe you want to stop being so available for the people that take advantage of you. Therefore, you can find more time for yourself.

What is it that you want to do more of? Is there something you're currently doing that you want to do more of? Maybe it's that you want to read more books. So, you go from reading one book every 3 months to reading 2 books in 3 months. You may want to expand your vocabulary. So, download a vocabulary app to your phone. To do more is to receive more.

What can you start doing? It's the choices that you make that really define you and can change anything in your life. It's wise to make better decisions. Maybe you want to start getting up earlier. So, you retire earlier in the evening. Maybe you want to live a healthier lifestyle. So, you change your eating habits and work out more. Stop talking about what you're going to do and just start doing it.

If you don't start to make some changes you choose to settle. It's just that simple. For some people they choose to settle. They truly feel there's nothing to change. They're happy with their lives. And that's fine for them. Maybe you're in a relationship that's dysfunctional. When you know you're not changing the dynamics of the relationship then you're choosing to settle with it. But if you want to be extraordinary and phenomenal and make an impact in people's lives, you have to do extraordinary and phenomenal things.

Action Steps

Grab your G.O.A.L. Digga Journal. I want you to answer each one of those questions. What do you want to do less of? What do you want to stop doing? What do you want to do more of? What do you want to start doing? Are you ready for a change?

"You don't have to see the entire staircase just take that first step" – Martin Luther King Jr.

20
What Does Success Mean to You

"If you don't design your own life plans, chances are you'll fall into someone else's plan. And guess what they have planned for you? Not much." Jim Rohn

Success means different things to different people. For some, success may mean achieving financial wealth or status, it may mean achieving a certain level of career success, and for others, it may mean personal fulfillment or happiness, or making a positive impact in the world. Finding what success means to you is an important part of setting and achieving your goals. To find what success means to you, consider the following steps:

1. **Reflect on your values:** Your values are the principles that guide your decisions and actions. Reflect on what is most important to you in life, and how achieving certain goals aligns with those values.

2. **Define your goals:** Write down your short-term and long-term goals and consider how achieving them will contribute to your definition of success. It's important to ensure that your goals align with your values and personal aspirations.

3. **Assess your strengths and weaknesses:** Understanding your strengths and weaknesses can help you set realistic goals and identify areas where you may need to improve to achieve success.

4. **Consider your passions:** Think about what activities or areas of interest make you feel most fulfilled and engaged. Pursuing your passions can be a key factor in achieving success on a personal level.

5. **Embrace your unique journey:** Remember that success is a personal journey, and it's important to embrace your own unique path. Don't compare yourself to others or measure your success based on external factors – focus on your own personal growth and achievements.

6. **Reassess your definition of success over time:** As you grow and change, your definition of success may evolve as well. Reassess your goals and values periodically to ensure that they still align with your personal definition of success.

Finding what success means to you is a personal journey that requires self-reflection, goal setting, and a clear understanding of your values, passions, and strengths. By taking the time to define your own personal definition of success, you can create a roadmap for achieving your goals and living a fulfilling life. Remember to embrace your unique journey, and don't be afraid to reassess your goals and priorities over time as you continue to grow and evolve.

Born in Detroit, Michigan, in 1951, Dr. Ben Carson grew up in a single-parent household with his mother, who had only a third-grade education. Despite his family's economic struggles and his own difficulties with academics, Carson set his sights on becoming a doctor from a young age. His hard work and determination paid off. After graduating from Yale University, he attended the University of Michigan Medical School, where he became the first African American to be named chief resident of neurosurgery. He went on to have a successful career as a neurosurgeon, performing groundbreaking surgeries and pioneering new techniques.

But Carson's definition of success went beyond his medical accomplishments. In his autobiography, *Gifted Hands*, Carson writes about his belief that success is not just about achieving personal goals, but about using one's talents to help others. He writes about the importance of education and of giving back to one's community.

Carson has lived out this philosophy in many ways. He has established the Carson Scholars Fund, which provides scholarships to students who demonstrate academic excellence and a commitment to community service. He has also been involved in numerous charitable organizations, including the Children's Miracle Network and the American Academy of Achievement.

In 2017, Carson was appointed by President Donald Trump as the Secretary of Housing and Urban Development. Despite facing criticism and controversy during his tenure, Carson remained committed to his vision of using his position to improve the lives of those in need.

Dr. Ben Carson's story is an inspiration to many, as it demonstrates the power of hard work, determination, and a commitment to serving others. He knew what success meant to him and worked tirelessly to achieve it, all while making a positive impact on the world around him.

What is success? According to the dictionary, it's the accomplishment of an aim or purpose. The favorable or prosperous termination of attempt or endeavors; the accomplishment of one's goal. The attainment of wealth, position, honors, or light. A performance of achievement that is marked by success, as by the attainment of honors.

Now what does that mean? For many, success means reaching a goal or accomplishing a task. Accomplishing what they set out to do. Something is considered a success when the outcome turns out well, is desired or favored.

One may say to have success you have to remain focused, be strategic, set measurable goals, revise when necessary, and manage your time. There are many philosophies about what success means. There are rules, keys, principles, and pillars to success to follow, according to certain philosophers. The important thing is what success means to you.

Answering the following questions honestly will help you set the goals that mean the most to you:

- What is your definition of success? Is it achieving material goals, great relationships, or spiritual awareness?

- Can you visualize your life after you achieve your goals? Remember, the more your success depends on the approval of others, the harder it will be to achieve and maintain.

- How does your definition of success affect you and those you care about most? For instance, if your goal is to get that coveted promotion, how will it affect the time you have for yourself and others?

- What drives or motivates you? What do you want to be recognized for? How much money would it take for you to be successful? Does it take winning to be successful for you? Is it power that you want?

- What satisfies you in your life? What achievements do you want? Is having balance between your personal life and professional life important to you?

Success can also mean freedom for you. You may want to do things your way without having to compromise. Like the saying goes, "Beauty is in the eye of the beholder." The same goes for success. Whatever success is, it's up to you to define it. Successful people don't get to where they are by following and pleasing people, we lead.

Action Steps

It's time to take out those G.O.A.L. Digga Journals again. I want you to write a list of the top 10 things you want in your life. It could be vacations, experiences, people that you want to meet, mastering a skill, or creating a business. Go big, remember this is about what you want. If you want an island, say that. Are you ready to create a vision of what success means to you?

"If you want to get the things most people don't have, you have to be willing to do the things most people won't do." – Unknown

21
Today Creates Tomorrow

Change is an inevitable part of life. Whether we like it or not, things are constantly changing around us, and it's up to us to adapt to those changes. But sometimes, we don't want to adapt - we want to make changes of our own. We want to improve our lives, achieve our goals, and create a better future for ourselves - that's where making changes today comes in.

Making changes today is all about taking action now to create a better tomorrow. It's about recognizing the areas of our lives that need improvement and taking steps to make those improvements happen. It's about being proactive instead of reactive and taking control of our own destiny.

So, how can we make changes today for a better tomorrow? Here are a few steps to get started:

- **Identify the areas of your life that need improvement:** The first step to making changes today is to identify the areas of your life that need improvement. This could be anything from your health and fitness to your career or relationships. Take some time to reflect on your life and make a list of the areas that you want to improve.

- **Set specific, achievable goals:** Once you've identified the areas of your life that need improvement, it's time to set some goals. Make sure your goals are specific, measurable, achievable, relevant, and time-bound (SMART). This will help you stay focused and motivated as you work towards achieving them.

- **Create a plan of action:** Now that you have your goals in place, it's time to create a plan of action. This could involve breaking your goals down into smaller, more manageable tasks, creating a schedule or routine, or seeking the help of a coach or mentor.

- **Take action today:** The most important step in making changes today is to take action now. Don't wait for tomorrow or next week - start taking steps towards your goals today. This could involve making small changes to your daily habits or taking bigger risks to pursue your dreams.

- **Stay committed and adaptable:** Making changes today is not always easy, and there will be obstacles and setbacks along the way. But it's important to stay committed to your goals and stay adaptable as you encounter challenges. Remember that change is a process, and it takes time and effort to see results.

Making changes today for a better tomorrow is all about taking action now to create the future you want. By identifying the areas of your life that need improvement, setting specific goals, creating a plan of action, taking action today, and staying committed and adaptable, you can make positive changes in your life and achieve your dreams. Remember, the future is in your hands - so start making changes today!

Barack Obama, born in Hawaii in 1961 to a Kenyan father and an American mother, grew up with a strong sense of social justice and a desire to make a positive impact on the world. As a young man, Obama struggled to find his place in the world. He grappled with questions of identity and purpose, and he faced numerous setbacks and disappointments along the way. But he never lost sight of his goal: to use his talents and abilities to make a difference in the world.

After graduating from college, Obama worked as a community organizer in Chicago, helping to empower residents of impoverished neighborhoods and bring about positive change. He then attended Harvard Law School, where he excelled academically and became the first Black president of the prestigious Harvard Law Review.

In 1996, Obama was elected to the Illinois State Senate, where he served for eight years before being elected to the United States Senate in 2004. During his time in the Senate, Obama became known for his enthusiastic advocacy on behalf of the disenfranchised and marginalized, and he earned a reputation as one of the most inspiring and eloquent speakers in American politics.

In 2008, Obama made history when he became the first Black President of the United States. He faced numerous challenges and obstacles during his time in office, but he remained committed to his vision of a more just and equitable society, and he worked tirelessly to bring about positive change.

Today, Barack Obama is widely regarded as one of the most inspirational and influential figures of our time. His life story is a testament to the power of perseverance, determination, and a belief in the transformative power of one's actions. Obama's story reminds us that we all have the power to shape our own destiny, and that every action we take today has the potential to create a better tomorrow.

Every morning you have to make a choice, either continue to sleep with your dream(s) or wake up and chase them. Every action you take today helps to create your future. So, ask yourself if any of your habits are an obstacle to reaching your goals.

Everything in your life happens for a reason. Your responsibility is to look at the things in your life and figure out why it is happening. You have that inner drive that you need to act on. You have to fight. Find that light within you and let it shine. I know it's a struggle, but you have to keep on scratching, kicking, and punching at those weaknesses and change them. Some days will be harder than others. You may not win all the time, still get up and start again.

Start today, not tomorrow. Activate your energy. Get out of bed and start your day with a grateful heart. Walk out that door knowing that you have to make better choices in your life. You have to start that chain reaction and once activated, it will allow you to keep going. It's the key to creating any kind of change. Why put something off for tomorrow when you can do it today?

It's almost like you have to be an addict, you have to be addicted to what you want. You have to believe in your passion and goals that much. You almost have to go crazy and be out of your mind to reach your goals. We all were designed with these talents and abilities to do this. So, anything you want in life you can accomplish. It's in your genetics. You were structured to be able to do great things. You are destined for greatness.

There is no difference between you and anyone you consider to be the ultimate model of success. You're capable of doing the same thing as anyone else. The only difference is they've learned to use their mind, body, and subconscious power on a consistent basis, effectively. You have yet to unlock it. Remember whatever we concentrate our focus on consistently, strive to learn from, and make new distinctions about, we will be great at.

I want to make this clear to you, you can do it. You can make that decision. No matter how difficult something may seem, you are able to figure it out. Go back to those daily routines and those nightly routines. Go back to your weekly plan. Take one step at a time, one day at a time, one week at a time. I don't care what has happened in your life, there is nothing that you cannot overcome. You have to know that the drive is within you.

What you do today will have an effect on tomorrow and everything you do in life. Have a continuous interest in improving yourself. Always be self-aware. Don't be afraid to put in the work. You're going to have to do the work, it's not going to be done for you. Never stop developing a passion for learning. Don't let anyone or anything deter you from being great. It begins right here, right now, today.

Action Steps

Today I want you to tell yourself you're in it to win it. Tell yourself that you will continue to accomplish the things you want in life and if you fail you will get up, brush yourself off, and do it over. Tell yourself you will continue even if no one else believes in it. This is your life, your journey. Tell yourself you are determined and will never give up. Repeat after me: I AM Powerful, I Am Strong, I AM Successful, I AM an Achiever, I AM Abundant, I AM Wealthy, I Am Focused, I AM Disciplined, I AM Healthy, I AM Wise, I AM Capable of Anything, I AM Someone that makes things Happen, I AM a Powerful Creator, I Am Grateful, I AM Ready, I AM a Fighter, I AM more than Enough, I AM a Champion. Remember to say this every day. You got this!

"Start now. Start where you are. Start with fear. Start with pain. Start with doubt. Start with hand shaking. Start with the voice trembling but start. Start and don't stop. Start where you are with what you have. Just start."
– Ijeoma Umebinyuo

22
Making a Desire Statement for Lifetime Goals

Writing a desire statement for lifetime goals can be a powerful tool for clarifying your aspirations and setting a clear direction for your life. Here are some steps to help you write a desire statement for your lifetime goals:

Start by reflecting on your core values, passions, and strengths. What are the things that matter most to you? What do you enjoy doing? What are you good at? What gives you a sense of purpose and fulfillment?

Consider your long-term vision for your life. What do you want to achieve? What kind of impact do you want to make? What kind of legacy do you want to leave behind?

Write down your desire statement using affirmative language that reflects your goals and aspirations. Be specific and concrete, and use vivid, descriptive language that brings your vision to life. For example, you might write: "I am living a life filled with adventure and creativity, where I am free to explore new places and ideas, and where I am constantly learning and growing."

Make your desire statement actionable by breaking it down into smaller, more manageable goals. Identify specific steps you can take to move closer to your desired outcome and create a plan to achieve those goals. Always revisit and revise your desire statement regularly, as your goals and priorities may evolve over time. Use it as a tool to stay focused and motivated, and to remind yourself of what you truly want out of life.

Mahatma Gandhi was born in 1869 in India and became a political and spiritual leader who advocated for nonviolent resistance and civil disobedience as a means of achieving independence for India. From a young age, Gandhi was driven by a deep desire to help his fellow Indians and to bring about positive change in the world. He was inspired by the teachings of his Hindu faith and by the example of other great leaders, such as Henry David Thoreau and Leo Tolstoy.

Throughout his life, Gandhi made a series of desired statements that guided his actions and helped him to stay focused on his goals. One of his most famous statements was, "Be the change you wish to see in the world." This simple yet powerful statement encapsulated Gandhi's belief that personal transformation was the key to creating positive social change.

Another desire statement that Gandhi made was, "The weak can never forgive. Forgiveness is the attribute of the strong." This statement reflects Gandhi's belief in the power of forgiveness and his conviction that it takes strength and courage to forgive those who have wronged us.

Gandhi's statements on desire were not just empty words - he lived them out in his daily life, using his actions to inspire and motivate others. His commitment to nonviolence and civil disobedience helped to galvanize the Indian independence movement and inspired countless others around the world to stand up for justice and freedom.

Today, Gandhi's legacy continues to inspire people all over the world to live their lives according to their own desire statements, to strive for personal transformation and positive social change, and to work towards a more peaceful and just world.

Writing down your goal and visualizing the outcome regularly will help you keep it in focus. Visualizing is a powerful technique for turning dreams into reality. Goals derived from the strategic planning process are provided structure and direction for more specific objectives. It's an objective or target that someone is trying to reach or achieve.

For example, you could write a goal that states: "I am saving enough money so I can retire early and open a spa in a beautiful location." That's a pretty good goal. Now, how are you going to structure that goal and give it direction? How are you going to breathe life into that goal? How can you visualize that goal?

You can think of an image that goes with the goal. Maybe a scenic countryside is the perfect location for your spa. Think of the different smells and the aroma that you want at your spa. Think of the chimes for the relaxing sounds you want at your spa. Or maybe the vision that motivates you is having a chocolate massage in your spa. How does it feel? Enjoy the moment with all your senses.

This exercise can also help you think of all those smaller goals that will create your lifetime goal. Fill in the important details: How much money will you need? How will you obtain those funds? How much money will you save per month and for how many months? What is the date that you are going to retire? What can you do each day to achieve your current tasks that propel you toward this goal?

Let's go over how to design your life and write your lifetime goals. There are going to be three parts. The design or the structure of your goals. Your habits or the action steps you put in place to achieve it. Following through or staying on track when you get off track. Following through is the main focus point. A lot of people fall off on this point.

The design is the vision. Go back to the Aspirational Vision that you wrote from Chapter 1. By now you should have a clear vision of what you want to design for your life. You have written those visions in your G.O.A.L. Digga Journal. You should take that journal with you everywhere you go. I don't know how many times when I'm out at a grocery store or over a friend's house and I think of a great idea, and by the time I got home I had forgotten it. That's why I want you to keep that journal with you so that you can always have a place to put your visions.

Figure out where you're at now, where you want to be, and are the habits you do every day getting you closer to your goal. You want to know what's working and what's not working. You want to know the barriers that are in the way and the direction you are moving towards.

You have daily habits. Think about the goals that you want to reach and break them down into daily habits. You want to lose 30 lbs. Don't worry about the pounds. Go for a walk every day and eat better. And again, it is very important to follow through. In case you didn't hear me I said, "FOLLOW THROUGH!" If you don't follow through and take action, how do you expect to get anything? If you want to get over the anxiety of speaking in public but refuse to network and talk to people at social events, how is that going to be possible?

Here is an example of a desire statement of my lifetime goals:

"I am committed to living a fulfilling and purposeful life by setting and achieving meaningful goals that align with my values and passions. I strive to continually grow and learn, to make a positive impact in the world, and to cultivate deep and meaningful relationships with those around me. I am determined to live a life that is authentic, joyful, and full of love, and to leave a lasting legacy that inspires others to pursue their own dreams and aspirations."

Action Steps

Join our live, in person, Zoom Accountability Call every Sunday at 8am central time, where we use our G.O.A.L. Digga Planner to plan our upcoming weekly goals and we also share resources. We post the live link in our Telegram, Facebook, and WhatsApp groups. Be sure to sign up for that.

"Goals give you more than a reason to get up in the morning; they are an incentive to keep you going all day. Goals tend to tap the deeper resources and draw the best out of life." – Harvey Mackay

23
Enthusiasm Counts

Enthusiasm is a powerful emotion that can provide a significant boost in achieving one's goals. When you are enthusiastic about something, you are filled with energy, motivation, and excitement. This positive energy can help you stay focused on your goal and maintain the persistence required to achieve it.

Here are some ways in which enthusiasm can help you achieve your goals:

- **Increases motivation:** When you are enthusiastic about a goal, you are more likely to be motivated to take action towards achieving it. You are more likely to work hard and put in the effort required to achieve your goal.
- **Boosts creativity:** Enthusiasm can help you tap into your creativity and come up with new ideas and solutions that can help you achieve your goal more effectively.

- **Improves focus:** When you are enthusiastic about something, you tend to be more focused and engaged. This can help you stay on track and avoid distractions that could derail your progress towards your goal.
- **Enhances perseverance:** Enthusiasm can help you stay committed to your goal, even when faced with challenges and setbacks. It can help you maintain a positive outlook and a belief in your ability to overcome obstacles and achieve your goal.

Overall, enthusiasm can be a powerful tool to help you achieve your goals. By staying enthusiastic it can help you to achieve success and lead a more fulfilling life. Having enthusiasm matters. It keeps you cheerful and happy. It makes you think of new and exciting ways to get things done. In anything you do, give it everything you got. When you have enthusiasm even the boring things seem to go by fast. You have to find the excitement within yourself and everything you do including achieving your goals.

Mae Jemison, the first African American woman to travel into space, was born in Decatur, Alabama, in 1956. From a young age, she developed a strong passion for science and space exploration. Jemison's enthusiasm for space was fueled by her love for *Star Trek*, a popular television series that depicted a future where people from diverse backgrounds worked together and explored the cosmos. She was inspired by the character Lieutenant Uhura, played by Nichelle Nichols, who was one of the first African American women to have a prominent role on a television show.

Jemison pursued her dreams with determination and unwavering enthusiasm. She excelled academically, earning a degree in chemical engineering from Stanford University and later attending Cornell University Medical College. After completing her medical studies, Jemison worked as a doctor in Los Angeles and traveled to developing countries to provide medical care.

In 1987, NASA announced its plans to recruit new astronauts, and Jemison seized the opportunity to apply. Despite facing numerous challenges and being one of only 15 candidates chosen out of over 2,000 applicants, Jemison's enthusiasm and determination shone through.

On September 12, 1992, Mae Jemison made history when she became the first African American woman to travel into space as a mission specialist on the space shuttle Endeavour. Her journey not only fulfilled her childhood dream but also symbolized a significant milestone for diversity and inclusion in space exploration.

Following her space mission, Jemison left NASA and dedicated her efforts to various ventures, including promoting STEM education and encouraging young people, particularly girls and minorities, to pursue careers in science and technology. She founded the Jemison Group, a technology consulting firm, and the Dorothy Jemison Foundation for Excellence, which supports educational initiatives.

Mae Jemison's story is a testament to the power of enthusiasm, perseverance, and breaking barriers. Her unyielding passion for space exploration and her tireless efforts to inspire and educate others serve as an inspiration to people around the world. Jemison's journey reminds us that enthusiasm can fuel our dreams and help us overcome obstacles on the path to achieving our goals.

Determine how you can make your goal easier to achieve. While some amount of sacrifice will be involved, your overall journey should be a pleasure as you look forward to the attainment of your dream. Put your whole soul into it. Great and epic things are achieved with enthusiasm.

One way of keeping the enthusiasm going is to reward yourself along the way. Even telling a supportive friend about a small achievement provides a sweet reward and a sense of pride. Maybe you could chart your progress and keep the sheet where you'll see it every day. Tape it to your mirror in the bathroom. Even if you're not reading it, it would be a reminder to your subconscious mind each time you walk into the bathroom.

You have to be intentional when having enthusiasm. Enthusiasm is that strong excitement of feeling you get. It is the fuel that drives things forward. Knowing you can achieve it with your clear vision in mind and your gratitude, it will come together. Enthusiasm is power. If you can control your enthusiasm you'll be able to control your experiences. You can turn your negative experiences into positive experiences.

How do you develop enthusiasm? I want to give you some ways for you to implement it into your life. You can do this in many ways. Have good posture, stand up strong and proud, and hold your head up and smile. Also, sometimes you have to say no to the people, places and activities in your life that drain your energy.

If you walk into an event with a great plan but you have no enthusiasm, who's going to pay attention to you? Who's going to believe you? You have to have that enthusiasm, that motivation, and that inspiration into what you're doing because you won't even believe yourself if you're not enthusiastic about what you're trying to do. But if you are enthusiastic, inspired, energetic, encouraged, excited, and motivated, then other people can pick up on that energy and it's contagious. You will be able to accomplish so much and achieve at a high level.

Action Steps

I want you to think of 10 things that you find dull or boring. I want you to find a way to smile about it and respond calmly. I want you to have a positive outlook on things that you may otherwise complain about. I also want you to be aware in your day-to-day activities of what may bother you and make it a point to see the better side of things. Can you keep the enthusiasm no matter what?

"A lion runs fastest when he is hungry." – Salman Khan

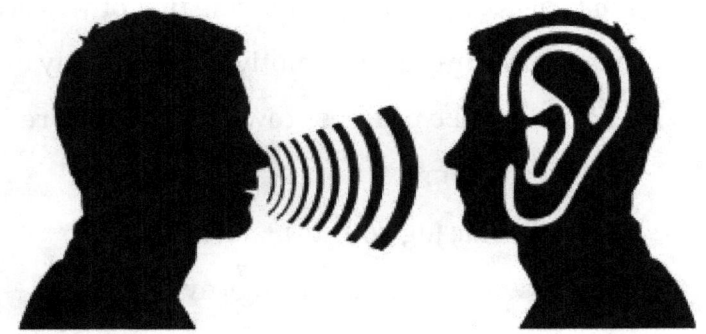

24
Let Others Know

Letting other people know about your transformation can be important for several reasons:

- **Accountability:** When you share your transformation journey with others, you create a sense of accountability. Knowing that others are aware of your goals can motivate you to stay on track and make progress towards your desired transformation.

- **Support:** Sharing your transformation journey with others can also provide you with emotional support. You may find that others have similar experiences and can offer advice or encouragement. Having a support system can also make the journey less lonely.

- **Inspiration:** Your transformation journey can inspire others to make positive changes in their own lives. Sharing your story can encourage others to take action and make positive changes, which can create a ripple effect of positivity.
- **Celebration:** When you reach your transformation goals, sharing your success with others can be a source of celebration and pride. Sharing your success with others can also motivate them to continue their own transformation journeys.

Overall, letting other people know about your transformation can help you stay accountable, provide emotional support, inspire others, and celebrate your successes. Let everyone know of your achievements and your goals. Don't try to downplay them. You try to be modest and try not to make the other person feel inadequate. It may even be because you have self-doubt. I know because I've done that. That's where it will hurt you so be true to yourself and others. Self-doubt can lead people to have a misconception of you. It can lead people to think you're not qualified. My point is, show excitement and confidence.

Anthony Robbins, born in 1960 in California, overcame a challenging upbringing and transformed his life through personal development and a commitment to helping others. In his early years, Robbins faced financial struggles and emotional turmoil. However, he discovered the power of self-improvement and began studying influential thinkers and motivational strategies. Inspired by his own transformation, Robbins developed a passion for empowering individuals and sharing his knowledge with others.

Robbins understood that personal growth was not just about transforming oneself but also about inspiring and positively impacting the lives of others. He believed that by letting others know about his own transformation and sharing his knowledge, he could help them achieve their goals and live more fulfilling lives. He started by organizing seminars and workshops where he shared his strategies for personal and professional success. His energetic and engaging speaking style resonated with people from all walks of life, and his message spread rapidly.

Through his books, including the best-selling "Awaken the Giant Within," Robbins reached a wider audience and became a renowned motivational speaker and life coach. His teachings focused on unlocking human potential, building self-confidence, and achieving lasting change.

One of Robbins' significant contributions was the creation of the "Firewalk Experience," where participants walk barefoot across hot coals to overcome fear and limiting beliefs. This transformative exercise became a metaphor for breaking through barriers and embracing personal transformation.

Robbins' willingness to share his own experiences of transformation and vulnerability inspired millions around the world to take charge of their lives and pursue their dreams. He emphasized the importance of seeking guidance and support from others on the path to success.

Today, Anthony Robbins, widely known as Tony Robbins, continues to impact lives through his books, seminars, and philanthropic efforts. He has worked with top athletes, business leaders, and individuals from diverse backgrounds, helping them unleash their potential and achieve extraordinary results.

Robbins' story reminds us of the significance of sharing our transformation with others. By being open and transparent about our own journey, we can inspire and empower those around us, forming a community of support and encouragement that propels us towards our goals.

I once thought being modest and being humble was a nice way to be. So, I sat in silence, not wanting to step on any toes. Until I was getting the short end of the stick and was looked over, walked on, and unnoticed. I soon learned that I wasn't getting the recognition I deserved. Worst of all, it made me look incompetent. I started wanting people to know that I was good at what I did. I am Intelligent. If you have gotten this far in this book I know that you want that too.

You may think your qualifications and achievements stand out. It may not be obvious to others. They may not automatically see it. It's not like you can wear it on your sleeve. So, you have to be verbal about it. Put it in their face where they can't miss it. Don't worry about repeating it over and over again. There's always someone that does not know about you and what you do. SAY IT LOUD!

We have been conditioned to think that if we're exciting and express it to people that we're bragging or we're boasting. In my opinion, if someone has something negative about what you're saying about your achievements, it's probably because they have nothing going on and are dealing with their own insecurities. What I'm saying is this, it's okay to be happy about the changes you're making in your life and letting other people know can be inspirational to the right person. So, continue to be great and let your light shine.

People will paint a picture in their mind about you from what you tell them. Sometimes you don't even have to say anything, people will have a perception of you and share their opinions with others. I know what you're thinking, I don't care what people think about me. In your everyday life I would say that's fine. But if you're an inspiring entrepreneur and a G.O.A.L. Digga and want to inspire people, they need to know the achievements you have made, otherwise why should anyone listen to you?

For instance, when going to apply for a job, a car loan, a credit card, or even a mortgage, do you want the underwriter to see unreliable information on your credit profile? Of course not, you want them to see that you have credit worthiness. You pay your bills on time; you keep your utilization low; you make more than enough money; and your Debt-To-Income ratio is where it needs to be. You care then, what they think about you. So, apply that to your achievements and goals. Let everyone as far as you can see know. How else are you going to get into the history books?

If other people are involved in the achievement of your goal, or if it's going to affect them, tell them about it so they may support you in your endeavors. If you need their help in any way, let them know. Being a part of a like-minded community is very powerful. My experience has been phenomenal because we all want each other to succeed. We support each other, we congratulate each other, and we believe in each other.

Action Steps

We are here for you, don't forget to tag G.O.A.L. Digga social media community and let us follow you on your journey. Let us know about the transformation you're going through. Let us know your WINS. We also want to know about your setbacks and how you overcame those obstacles. That helps other G.O.A.L. Diggas in our community. Share with us any challenges you're facing and let us know how we can assist you.

"People like to look around or wait for someone to stand up; for someone who can help; someone who can make a difference. Very rarely do people look at themselves, you can be that someone." - Unknown

25
Be Prepared for Setbacks

Setting goals and pursuing them is a common human aspiration. However, the journey to achieve your goals can be unpredictable, and setbacks are inevitable. Therefore, being prepared for setbacks is essential to maintain motivation and avoid giving up on your goals.

One of the first steps in preparing for setbacks is to anticipate them. By anticipating setbacks, you can plan and strategize how to deal with them when they arise. It's essential to identify potential obstacles, such as time constraints, lack of resources, or unexpected challenges, and develop a plan to overcome them.

Another important step is to build resilience. Resilience is the ability to bounce back from setbacks and continue pursuing your goals. Building resilience requires cultivating a growth mindset, accepting that setbacks are a natural part of the journey and using them as an opportunity to learn and grow. Instead of giving up when things go wrong, you should use setbacks as a chance to refine our approach and find new solutions to overcome the obstacle.

It's also crucial to surround yourself with supportive people who can offer encouragement, motivation, and guidance when facing setbacks. Having a support system can help you maintain your momentum and keep you focused on your goals. It's also essential to seek out resources and information that can help you overcome setbacks. Whether it's reading a book, attending a workshop, or seeking advice from a mentor, you should actively seek out tools that can help you overcome obstacles.

It's essential to maintain a positive outlook and keep a long-term perspective. Setbacks can be discouraging, but it's crucial to remember that success is rarely achieved overnight. It takes time, effort, and perseverance to achieve your goals, and setbacks are an inevitable part of that journey. By keeping a positive outlook and focusing on the bigger picture, you can stay motivated and continue to work towards your goals, even when faced with setbacks.

Ursula Burns, the former CEO of Xerox, was raised in a housing project in New York City, Burns faced numerous obstacles throughout her life. However, she refused to let those setbacks define her, and instead, used them as motivation to work harder and achieve her goals.

After graduating from college, Burns began working as a summer intern at Xerox, where she quickly worked her way up the corporate ladder. However, she faced discrimination and sexism along the way, with some colleagues suggesting that she was only given opportunities because of affirmative action. Despite these setbacks, Burns continued to excel in her career, eventually becoming the first Black woman to lead a Fortune 500 company when she was appointed as CEO of Xerox in 2009.

Throughout her career, Burns stressed the importance of being prepared for setbacks. She knew that obstacles were inevitable, but rather than letting them hold her back, she used them as opportunities to learn and grow.

In an interview with Forbes, Burns said, "You have to prepare for the fact that things are going to go wrong, but you have to also prepare for the fact that things are going to go right. And you have to be able to ride both of those waves."

Another amazing person who knew of setbacks was Madam C.J. Walker, a self-made millionaire who became one of the most successful African American businesswomen in the early 20th century. Born Sarah Breedlove in 1867, Walker was the daughter of former slaves and grew up in poverty. She was orphaned at a young age and married at 14 but was widowed by the age of 20 with a young daughter to support. She worked as a laundress and lived in extreme poverty for several years, until she discovered a hair care formula that would change her life.

Walker began to experiment with various hair products and eventually developed a formula that helped promote hair growth and scalp health for African American women. She began selling her product door-to-door, and within a few years, her business had grown exponentially. She eventually founded the Madam C.J. Walker Manufacturing Company, which employed thousands of saleswomen across the country and made her one of the wealthiest women in America.

Despite her success, Walker faced many setbacks and obstacles along the way. She was initially rejected by many investors and faced racism and discrimination as a Black woman in a male-dominated business world. However, she remained resilient and was always prepared for setbacks.

Walker was a firm believer in education and self-improvement. She attended business school and hired consultants to help her improve her marketing and sales strategies. She also established a beauty school to train her saleswomen and help other African American women achieve financial independence.

Throughout her life, Walker remained committed to helping others and advocating for civil rights. She used her wealth and influence to support various causes, including the National Association for the Advancement of Colored People (NAACP) and scholarships for African American students.

Burns' and Walker's legacy continues to inspire many people today. Both proved that with hard work, perseverance, and a willingness to learn and adapt, anyone can achieve their goals and overcome setbacks.

Setbacks are a natural part of pursuing your goals, and being prepared for them is essential to stay motivated and avoid giving up. By anticipating setbacks, building resilience, surrounding ourselves with supportive people, seeking out resources and information, and maintaining a positive outlook, we can overcome setbacks and continue to make progress towards our goals. Remember, setbacks are not failures, but opportunities to learn and grow.

Setbacks are going to happen, so you have to be prepared. It's what you do when you encounter setbacks that matters. Are you going to be a quitter? You can feel disappointed and discouraged when you don't reach a goal, however, you can't give up. You're going to have to stay committed. Don't be a quitter. Everything is not going to always go as planned.

Make sure you set realistic expectations. You want to always think positively about your goals and believe in your ability to succeed, however, don't expect everything to go perfectly or even easily all the time. Most goals that are worth achieving require time, effort and perseverance. Aim high but always know that a step back is not the end of the world. There's always a way to get to where you're going from where you are, so don't get disappointed, get motivated.

Again, planning is very helpful in preparing for setbacks. Roadblocks will come. Being prepared in advance increases your chances of quickly and easily tackling the detours around it. You must find a way around those roadblocks so consider what obstacles could hold you back and plan for them now.

When you're looking back at a goal you set and realize that you failed to reach your goal, why do you think that was? What happened, what held you back, what else could have been done, what are you going to do to make sure that this doesn't happen again? Being able to reflect and assess what could go wrong will help you change it.

Learning to be flexible will help you with setbacks. Recognize in planning, sometimes emergencies happen and priorities change. Since you know that obstacles will happen you have to be willing to be flexible. Especially when planning further than 60 days in the future, plans will certainly change. So, it's okay if you don't get all your daily or weekly tasks done or don't reach your month's expectation. Sometimes you have to go with the flow.

That feeling you get when you get drawn to an activity and get lost in it and you could do it for hours and hours at a time. That's the most productive and enjoyable time. So, allow yourself to follow your bliss and at least always know that setbacks are not the end of the world. There's always a way to reroute to your goal from where you are.

Be open to lessons and blessings. There is a saying that goes: "When you make plans, God laughs." So, even if you're not religious, this phrase has an important point. It's not that someone else is making a plan for you, it's that what you want comes to you in ways you may not expect. Sometimes you get rerouted to a goal that turns out to be better than you expected. Know that sometimes a setback is exactly what you need to learn to really get you in the right place. Maybe showing the weakness in your plan, giving you an opportunity to improve, or even dream bigger. It may even inspire a new goal. Stay committed and know what things might set you back so you can tackle them now.

Sometimes those close to you may find it challenging to understand why you're working so hard to achieve your goals. They mean well, but they may be struggling with their own goals. This could manifest in words and actions you may find discouraging. Jealousy is another possibility. Just be aware of these realities and keep a positive outlook on your journey. Be prepared to stand on your own feet and rely on yourself instead of your loved ones for support.

Action Steps

Go back to the goals that you set for yourself; I want you to think of any setback that might get in your way. I want you to prepare for various obstacles that can arise. I don't want you to write negative things like, "I may not come up with the money." I'm talking about obstacles that are out of your reach, that you may have no control over. If it is money issues, find a solution. Things like, how to increase your income to purchase supplies for your business. Can you prepare for that?

"People are like tea bags, you find out how strong they are when you put them in hot water"

– Unknown

26
Take Your Time

In today's fast-paced world, it's easy to get caught up in the rush of achieving your goals. You often set your sights on a particular objective and push yourself to achieve it as quickly as possible, without taking the time to consider whether it's truly the right path for you. However, taking time with your goals is crucial to ensuring that you pursue the right objectives in the right way.

When you take the time to reflect on your goals, you gain clarity on what you truly want to achieve and why it's important to you. You can then identify the steps needed to achieve those goals, as well as potential roadblocks that may arise along the way. This allows you to develop a well-thought-out plan that takes into account your strengths, weaknesses, and personal values.

Moreover, taking time with your goals allows you to consider the impact they may have on your lives and those around you. You can ask yourselves questions like, "Will achieving this goal bring me happiness and fulfillment?" or "Will pursuing this goal harm others in any way?" By considering these factors, you can ensure that your goals align with your personal values and contribute positively to your life and society.

It's important to note that taking time with your goals doesn't necessarily mean you need to slow down or take a passive approach. Rather, it's about taking a deliberate and thoughtful approach, rather than rushing into things without proper consideration. You can still pursue your goals with energy and enthusiasm, but with a more measured and thoughtful approach.

Additionally, taking time with your goals allows you to embrace the process of achieving them. When you rush towards a goal, you may become so focused on the end result that you overlook the journey along the way. However, by taking the time to enjoy the process of achieving your goals, you can derive greater satisfaction from the experience and appreciate the growth and learning that takes place along the way.

Taking time with your goals is essential to ensuring that you pursue the right objectives in the right way. By taking a deliberate and thoughtful approach, you can develop well-thought-out plans that align with your personal values and positively impact your life and society. It's important to remember that the journey towards achieving your goals is just as important as the end result, and taking time with your goals allows you to appreciate and enjoy the process.

Warren Buffett, one of the world's most successful investors and philanthropists, is known for his methodical approach to investing, which involves careful analysis and patience. He famously said, "The stock market is a device for transferring money from the impatient to the patient." Buffett is also known for his long-term thinking and focus on value investing - buying high-quality companies at a reasonable price and holding onto them for the long haul.

Buffett's success is not just due to his investment strategy, but also his ability to reflect on his goals and values. In his early years as an investor, Buffett worked for legendary investor Benjamin Graham, who taught him the importance of "margin of safety" - buying assets at a discount to their intrinsic value in order to minimize risk. But as Buffett's career progressed, he realized that he needed to go beyond just investing for profit. He began to focus on investing in companies that had a positive impact on society and that aligned with his personal values. He also became a major philanthropist, giving away billions of dollars to causes such as education and poverty reduction.

Throughout his career, Buffett has emphasized the importance of taking your time and not rushing into decisions. He famously said, "We don't have to be smarter than the rest. We have to be more disciplined than the rest." He also advises young people to take time to reflect on their goals and values before making major life decisions.

Overall, Warren Buffett's life and career serve as an inspiration for anyone who wants to achieve success while staying true to their values and taking a patient, reflective approach to decision-making.

It's understandable if you want to try to achieve your goals as quickly as possible, but patience and persistence is what wins the day. I'm not saying to take a small goal that typically takes you 2 days to complete and stretch it out for a month. I'm talking about those big bodacious goals that may take 6 to 9 months. Taking small steps and building on each small victory leads to more lasting changes. You know what they say, "Rome was not built in a day."

You have to have time for the other important things in your life. Achieving your goals is not a Sprint, it's a marathon. You want to be able to have the time it takes to conquer that goal. Your life consists of so many different things. You have to have room for your day-to-day operations and duties as well. You may have to work, go to school, raise a family, and so much more. You don't want to overwhelm yourself with having a short time frame for something that takes longer to accomplish.

You can change course or make adjustments on the way if something unexpected turns up or if things go differently than you envisioned. I've mentioned this several times throughout this book. It's essential for you to know there is no perfect way to do things. Especially when following someone else's blueprint, although it worked for them in a particular way, it may not work the same way for you. So, it's okay to make those necessary adjustments to fit your own circumstances.

You'll enjoy your journey because you'll have the time to pause and celebrate your small achievement. This is the fun part, completing the things you set forth to do and checking it off as completed. Like I said before, it gives you a sense of accomplishment, a sense of worthiness, like there's nothing that you can't achieve. You feel so empowered. When you celebrate, that just gives you a boost of enthusiasm and adrenaline to complete the next goal.

You're more likely to be stress free by putting less pressure on yourself. When you put the right time frame in place to accomplish your goals, you have a sense of relief. You're not going to feel rushed. Now sometimes a little pressure can be good when you're trying to challenge yourself. So don't take it for granted that you have all the time in the world. You want to have a balance with just enough pressure to keep you motivated but not so much that it stresses you.

The point that I'm making is this: Reaching those bigger goals is all about a steady step-by-step process. Taking one step at a time and adjusting your goals along the way is essential to progress. Remember that you do have other responsibilities in life that are just as important as achieving your goals. Make sure you celebrate each milestone that you achieve along the way. Most importantly, stay positive and show gratitude.

Action Steps

Go to your G.O.A.L Digga Planner and evaluate your goals. Make an assessment to be sure you gave yourself enough time to attain your goals. If the time frame works out for you, leave it the way it is. But keep in mind that you can always go back and readjust them. Did you set the right amount of time for your goals? Also join G.O.A.L. Digga on Clubhouse where we converse and give our testimonies.

"All dreams are within reach; all you have to do is keep moving." – Unknown

27
Always Keep Your Goal in Sight

Goals are the foundation of success. They give us direction, purpose, and motivation to achieve what we desire. However, it can be challenging to stay focused on our goals amidst the distractions and pressures of daily life. In this chapter, we'll explore some strategies to help you keep your goals in sight and achieve them.

Write Down Your Goals - One of the most effective ways to keep your goals in sight is to write them down. This simple act will help you clarify what you want to achieve and make it easier to remember. Write down your goals in your G.O.A.L. Digga planner and keep them where you can see them every day. You can also create a vision board with pictures and words that represent your goals.

Break Them Down - Big goals can feel overwhelming and make it difficult to take action. To make it easier, break them down into smaller, manageable tasks. Create a list of steps you need to take to achieve your goal and focus on one task at a time. Celebrate each accomplishment and keep moving forward.

Visualize Your Success - Visualization is a powerful tool that can help you stay motivated and focused on your goals. Take a few minutes every day to imagine yourself achieving your goal. See yourself doing what you set out to do, and feel the emotions associated with success. This practice will help you stay inspired and committed to your goal.

Set Deadlines - Deadlines are a great way to keep yourself accountable and stay on track. Set specific deadlines for each task or milestone and make a commitment to meet them. This approach will help you break your goal into manageable pieces, and it will also help you avoid procrastination.

Make a Plan - Having a plan is essential for achieving your goals. Create a roadmap that outlines the steps you need to take to reach your goal and set milestones along the way. Use your G.O.A.L. Digga planner or to track your progress, and adjust your plan as needed.

Find Support - Achieving your goals can be a challenging journey. Having a support system can make all the difference. Share your goals with friends, family, or a mentor, and ask for their support and encouragement. Join a community of like-minded individuals who are also working towards similar goals.

Keeping your goals in sight is essential to achieving success. By following these strategies, you can stay motivated, focused, and committed to your goals. Remember that achieving your goals is a journey, not a destination. Celebrate each accomplishment, learn from setbacks, and keep moving forward.

Amanda Gorman is a young teenage poet and activist, who gained national attention after reciting her poem "The Hill We Climb" at President Joe Biden's inauguration in January 2021.

Growing up in Los Angeles, Amanda faced many obstacles on her path to success. She struggled with a speech impediment and was diagnosed with a neurological condition that made reading difficult. Despite these challenges, Amanda was determined to pursue her passion for writing and poetry.

At the age of 16, Amanda became the first Youth Poet Laureate of Los Angeles, and later went on to become the first National Youth Poet Laureate in 2017. Her poetry is known for its powerful messages of hope, unity, and social justice.

Through her work, Amanda has shown the importance of setting goals and persevering in the face of adversity. She has also become a role model for young people, particularly Black teenage girls, who may face obstacles and discrimination in pursuing their dreams.

In an interview with NPR, Amanda said, "My hope is that my words will inspire and uplift people, and that they'll feel empowered to make change in their own communities." Her commitment to using her talents for the greater good is a testament to the power of setting and achieving one's goals, no matter the challenges.

You are a hero! You've set out to achieve something important to you and you already possess the integrity and courage to see it through. Of course, on your heroic journey, you just might find yourself going off track once in a while. That's completely normal. Just always remember your why. Why are you doing this? You know you're tired of getting those same results so it's up to you to do different things. The things you're doing now are not getting what you want.

Maybe you'll feel disheartened when you're tested (like all heroes are). At these times, remember that all happy and successful people have goals and challenges. You deserve to lead the life you've dreamed of. So don't let the challenges scare you. How many times did you fall when you were a baby learning to walk? Many. How many times did you stop? Never. It's the same principle, don't give up on it and it won't give up on you. Tell yourself you're going to do this, tell yourself you're going to stick to it.

At every milestone you reach, review your progress to keep yourself motivated. Instead of allowing setbacks to derail you, allow them to correct your course. Allow small victories to propel you forward to the future you deserve. A turtle and a giraffe will never see eye to eye. The turtle can only see so far because he's always on the ground. But the giraffe whose head is high in the sky can see so much further. I want to say a bird can see broader. All of us have the hero within us, waiting to be discovered. Effectively setting goals that matter leads you to becoming the best you that you can be, and enjoying the happy life you deserve.

If you could be focused on completing the steps that get you to your destiny, there's nothing you can't do. You have to understand, in doing that, it will open up doors for so much more. Then you go through that door and more doors open, and before you know it "Infinity." The doors are endless. In other words, the opportunities are endless. You just need to plan which way to go next and follow those steps. Then what else do you want?

You have to be able to concentrate on your efforts. When you're able to concentrate, you will become a true G.O.A.L. Digga. Nothing will be able to distract you. Nothing and no one can stop you. You know what to do, you know how to do it, so you do it. There's no such thing as obstacles, only solutions. You don't see any barriers. You're focused on the outcome, and you're going to concentrate and do what it takes until you get there. You are unstoppable!

I'm going to end with this, you don't have to win or become successful in your life. You don't have to inspire anyone. You don't have to be a productive citizen. You don't have to give back. You don't have to do anything that's not required of you to do. That's why you don't see many people become successful. Because no one wants to do anything, they don't want to do the work. You have to have discipline and make sacrifices to be in the room with success. You can't compete with someone that is driven. You can't compete with someone with a desire. You can't compete with someone that is focused and knows how to concentrate. You have to be a G.O.A.L. Digga to do "DAT."

Action Steps

I want you to take the next 3 months and really focus and concentrate on your desires and your goals that you are going to complete within that time frame. You should not be watching your television, or on social media unless it's building your brand. You should let your friends know that you will be unavailable, not hanging out, or spending hours on the phone chatting with them. Let your family know you love them, but you have things to do right now. Can you stay focused and concentrate without worry?

"Knowing is not enough, we must apply. Willing is not enough, we must do. The most dangerous person is the one who listens, thinks, and observes." – *Bruce Lee*

28
Avoid Temptation

Temptation can be a powerful force that distracts us from our goals and leads us astray. Whether it's the temptation to indulge in unhealthy habits or to procrastinate when we have important tasks to do, it's important to develop strategies to resist temptation and stay on track. In this chapter, we'll explore some practical ways to avoid temptation and stay focused on our goals.

Identify Your Triggers: The first step in avoiding temptation is to identify your triggers. What situations or emotions tend to lead you towards temptation? Is it boredom, stress, or social pressure? Once you know your triggers, you can create a plan to avoid them or mitigate their impact.

Change Your Environment: This can be an effective way to avoid temptation. If you're trying to avoid unhealthy food, remove it from your home and stock up on healthy options instead. If social media distracts you from important tasks, consider deleting apps from your phone or using software to limit your access.

Practice Mindfulness: Mindfulness is the practice of being present and fully engaged in the current moment. When we're mindful, we're less likely to get caught up in thoughts or emotions that lead us towards temptation. Try incorporating mindfulness practices into your daily routine, such as meditation or yoga.

Use Positive Self-Talk: Positive self-talk is a powerful tool that can help you resist temptation. When you feel the urge to give in, remind yourself of your goals and the reasons why you're pursuing them. Use affirmations to reinforce positive self-talk, such as "I am strong and capable of achieving my goals."

Plan Ahead: Planning ahead can help you avoid temptation by reducing the number of decisions you have to make at the moment. For example, if you're trying to eat healthier, plan your meals and snacks ahead of time. If you're trying to avoid procrastination, create a schedule that outlines your tasks for the day.

Find Support: Having a support system can help you stay accountable and resist temptation. Share your goals with friends or family members who can offer encouragement and support. Join a support group or online community of individuals who share similar goals.

David Goggins, a retired Navy SEAL and ultramarathon runner, grew up in a difficult environment, facing poverty, racism, and abuse. As a young adult, he worked as a pest control technician before joining the military. During his time as a Navy SEAL, Goggins completed multiple deployments and earned numerous awards for his bravery and service.

After leaving the military, Goggins became an ultramarathon runner, completing some of the world's most challenging races, including the Badwater Ultramarathon, the Western States 100-Mile Endurance Run, and the Moab 240.

Goggins is known for his incredible mental toughness and ability to push through pain and adversity. He credits his success to his ability to avoid distractions and temptations that could interfere with his goals. He once said, "Motivation is crap. Motivation comes and goes. When you're driven, whatever is in front of you will get destroyed."

Despite facing numerous setbacks and injuries throughout his career, Goggins has continued to push himself to new heights. He emphasizes the importance of staying focused on one's goals and avoiding distractions that can derail one's progress.

Through his example, Goggins shows that success is not just about talent or physical ability, but also about discipline, determination, and the ability to resist temptation and distractions. His story serves as an inspiration to anyone striving to achieve their goals, no matter how difficult the journey may be.

Avoiding temptation is essential for achieving our goals and staying on track. By identifying our triggers, changing our environment, practicing mindfulness, using positive self-talk, planning ahead, and finding support, we can develop effective strategies to resist temptation and stay focused on our goals. Remember that it's okay to stumble along the way - what's important is that we keep moving forward towards our goals.

You know that eating right and exercising are the path to your goal, so find ways to build support so you avoid temptation. You can have someone remind you to get up early in the morning and take an alternate route that steers you away from the bakery, for example. Or you can choose a sweet fruit such as grapes, strawberries, or apples when you are grocery shopping that is a better snack choice.

This is how most successful people achieve their goals. They avoid situations that would lead them to temptation. If you do give in, get back on track without self-recrimination and, instead, be determined to make a better choice next time. There is no need to blame yourself and beat yourself up about setbacks. When you give into temptation, that desire to do something wrong or unwise complicates things.

You must remove temptation. To do this, you have to have self-discipline. If you are trying to lose weight, or if you are trying to do better in life, you have to remove the temptations that hold you back from keeping your word to yourself. You have to have self-control, the willpower over your basic desires is what you want to get under control. You start by changing your habits. One way of changing your habits is changing your environment as mentioned before. Go to different places, be around different people, and do different things. The things you do should be things that's going to add value to your life and give you a sense of purpose.

I had a problem for years with hanging around with the wrong people doing the wrong things. In my younger years I went to house parties. I'm not saying anything is wrong with the house party, but as I got older I started hanging out at bootleggers' houses. I'm so thankful I was not an alcoholic; I just loved the social atmosphere of a house party. I kind of got addicted to going. The environment was not a good environment. Mostly everyone there didn't have any goals, was there every day of the week, and had no aspiration to do anything in life.

It was one of those temptations I had to eliminate. I started going there every weekend like clockwork. I didn't have any goals or aspirations either at the time. I had to evaluate my life and get on the right path. I tried to stop. But every Friday night I made my way right back to that house. I couldn't avoid the temptation. I knew when those feelings were coming. I had to change my lifestyle. I started wanting more in life. I started going around different people that influenced me in better ways. I had to avoid the people and places that are not bringing value to my life.

Now, I still get to experience the social environment, except now, its seminars, conventions, and conferences. And after those events we sometimes have a ball or some sort of celebration. So, I'm still getting what I want just in a different, more positive way.

Action Steps

Take out your G.O.A.L. Digga Journal and write down some of your temptations that you should eliminate in your life. What are some of the things that you have been struggling with? Write down on one side of your Journal your old habits (the ones not benefiting where you want to go) and the other side write the new habits you want to implement. How can you avoid temptation? If you need more support go to our website www.goaldigga.org and join the G.O.A.L. Digga Boot Camp.

"Your thoughts become your words, your words become your actions, your actions become habits, your habits become character. character is who you are and determines your past in life. You make your own destiny."
– Unknown

29
Self-Discipline

Self-discipline is a vital skill that plays a significant role in our personal and professional lives. It's the ability to control our thoughts, emotions, and behaviors to achieve our goals, even when faced with obstacles or distractions. Self-discipline is essential because it enables us to make progress towards our goals, develop healthy habits, and achieve success. In this chapter, we'll explore the importance of self-discipline and how it can benefit us in various areas of life.

One of the most significant benefits of self-discipline is that it helps you achieve your goals. When you have self-discipline, you can stay focused and motivated towards your goals, even when you face challenges or setbacks. You can create a plan, manage your time effectively, and avoid distractions that can hinder your progress. With self-discipline, you can break down your goals into smaller, manageable steps and take consistent action towards achieving them.

It's essential for developing healthy habits. Whether it's eating healthily, exercising regularly, or getting enough sleep, self-discipline enables you to make positive choices that promote your physical and mental wellbeing. You can resist temptation and avoid unhealthy behaviors that can harm your health and wellbeing.

It's a key factor in enhancing productivity. When you have self-discipline, you can manage your time effectively and avoid procrastination. You can prioritize your tasks and focus on the most important ones first, avoiding distractions that can waste your time and energy. With self-discipline, you can accomplish more in less time, which can lead to greater success and fulfillment.

Having self-discipline can improve your relationships with others. When you have self-discipline, you can control your emotions and avoid reacting impulsively. You can communicate effectively, listen actively, and resolve conflicts constructively. With self-discipline, you can cultivate positive relationships based on respect, trust, and mutual understanding.

It helps in achieving success in all areas of life. Whether it's personal or professional success, self-discipline enables you to overcome challenges and persevere towards your goals. It helps you develop the habits and behaviors necessary for success, such as hard work, dedication, and persistence.

Self-discipline is a crucial skill that plays a significant role in your personal and professional lives. It enables you to achieve your goals, develop healthy habits, enhance productivity, improve relationships, and achieve success. By developing self-discipline, you can cultivate the habits and behaviors necessary to lead a fulfilling and successful life.

Les Brown is a renowned motivational speaker, author, and former Ohio State legislator who has inspired millions of people with his powerful messages of personal development and self-motivation. Born in an impoverished neighborhood in Miami, Florida, Les Brown faced numerous challenges and setbacks in his early life. He was labeled as educable mentally retarded (EMR) in school and faced the limitations and prejudices associated with that label. However, Les refused to let those circumstances define him or limit his potential.

At the age of 18, Les was inspired by a speech given by the renowned speaker, Zig Ziglar. This experience ignited a spark within him and awakened his desire to become a speaker himself. With little education and no formal training, Les embarked on a journey to transform his life and achieve his dreams.

Through sheer determination and unwavering self-discipline, Les worked on honing his speaking skills, studying successful speakers, and continuously developing himself. He immersed himself in personal development materials and motivational books, shaping his mindset and strengthening his belief in his own abilities.

Les faced numerous rejections and failures along the way, but he persisted, learning from each setback, and using them as steppingstones towards his goals. His self-discipline allowed him to maintain focus on his vision and push through the obstacles that stood in his path.

Eventually, Les' relentless efforts paid off. He became a highly sought-after speaker, captivating audiences with his charismatic presence, powerful storytelling, and motivational messages. Les's speeches have touched the lives of countless individuals, empowering them to unleash their full potential and achieve greatness.

Throughout his career, Les Brown has stressed the importance of self-discipline in achieving success. He encourages individuals to take responsibility for their actions, stay committed to their goals, and maintain a relentless work ethic. Les believes that self-discipline is the key to unlocking one's true potential and achieving extraordinary results.

Les Brown's journey from a disadvantaged background to becoming a globally recognized motivational speaker is a testament to the transformative power of self-discipline. His story serves as an inspiration for anyone striving to accomplish their goals, showing that with unwavering discipline and belief in oneself, anything is possible.

Setting big, complex goals is a powerful way to ensure you'll always keep your goals in sight and attain them. It's crazy, 95% of people are not willing to do what it takes to make their dreams come true. If you want to bring any of your goals into fruition you must have self-discipline. I don't want you to look at discipline as a punishment. Look at it as correcting one's actions for the sake of improvement. I believe self-discipline is the definition of self-love.

But what is self-love? Self-love is when you want to eat those sweets and junk food, but you tell yourself, "I love myself too much to let myself do that." Self-love is when you stop going back to a dysfunctional relationship because you love yourself that much. Self-love is when it's a Saturday night and you want to go out with all your friends and party, but you know you have to get up in the morning and get different tasks done to better your life. Because if you don't you're not going to feel good about yourself, so you say, "I love me too much to go out tonight."

If you want to be happy, you have to love yourself. In other words, you have to dissipate your behavior. We tend to base our self-esteem on what other people think. Self-esteem is how you feel about yourself. It has nothing to do with anyone else. It's not healthy to allow other people to determine how you're going to feel about yourself. Other people's opinions are just their opinions. It does not define you. You have to remember broken people want you broken. Sad people want you sad. Angry people want you to be angry. So, you cannot rely on someone else's opinion of you.

Whose fault do you think it is if something is broken within yourself? It's no one else's fault. It's your responsibility to fix it. For example, I can complain about my upbringing and how I was raised; How I didn't think I was treated fairly as a child. That I was the black sheep of the family. It's not my fault how I was raised. I am obligated to take ownership and it's my responsibility to figure out how I'm going to deal with those traumas and make a life for myself. I have to take that pain and overcome it and build happiness for myself, not complain about it.

I know it hurts. It's not your fault. It's not my fault. When something is somebody's fault you want them to be punished. You want them to hurt, and you want them to pay for what they've done. You want them to fix it. But that's not how it works. Most of the time they don't care, they're hurting themselves, and they can't even fix themselves. This is your life, happiness, peace of mind, and your responsibility alone.

As long as you keep pointing fingers and continue to be stuck on whose fault something is, you will forever be a victim. Why keep putting yourself through that? Stop making yourself suffer. Start nourishing yourself. You don't have any time to waste.

Action Steps

Look at your last 5 text messages. Are the people feeding your flames or dowsing your fire? Think about the people you have around you, are they powering you up, or sucking the life out of you? Sometimes in order to change your life you have to change your circle. Build new relationships. Let go of destructive people in your life. Add 5 new encouraging people to your contact list. Sometimes changing your circle will change your life. Do you want change?

"You have to set goals that are almost out of reach. If you set a goal that is attainable without much work or thought, you are stuck with something below your true talent and potential." – Steve Garvey

30
Join Others with Similar Goals

Joining others with similar goals can be incredibly important for achieving success and fulfillment in various aspects of life. Whether it's a personal goal, a professional aspiration, or a social cause, connecting with like-minded individuals can offer a range of benefits that can make a significant difference in the outcome.

One of the most notable benefits of joining others with similar goals is the sense of community and support that can be gained. When you surround yourself with people who share your vision and ambition, you have the opportunity to exchange ideas, learn from each other's experiences, and gain valuable insights into how to achieve your goals more effectively.

Moreover, having a support network of people who understand your struggles and can offer encouragement and motivation can help you stay focused and committed to your goals, even in difficult times.

Another benefit of joining others with similar goals is the potential for collaboration and partnership. By working together with others who share your vision, you can leverage each other's strengths and resources to achieve your goals more efficiently and effectively. Whether it's pooling resources, sharing knowledge and expertise, or dividing tasks and responsibilities, working in a team can help you achieve greater results than you could on your own.

Joining others with similar goals can provide opportunities for growth and learning. When you surround yourself with people who have similar interests and aspirations, you can gain exposure to new perspectives, ideas, and approaches that can broaden your horizons and expand your knowledge base. By interacting with others who are passionate about the same things as you, you can challenge your assumptions, refine your thinking, and gain new insights that can help you achieve your goals more effectively.

When you join others with similar goals it can provide a sense of purpose and belonging. When you align yourself with a community of people who share your values and aspirations, you can feel like you are part of something bigger than yourself. This can be especially important when pursuing social or environmental causes that require collective action to make a meaningful impact. By joining forces with others who share your passion, you can amplify your voice and make a more significant contribution to the causes you care about.

Eric Thomas, also known as ET the Hip Hop Preacher. He is a renowned motivational speaker, author, and educator, who has made a significant impact on individuals seeking personal and professional transformation. His journey is a testament to the power of joining forces with like-minded individuals. Born into a challenging environment in Detroit, Michigan, Eric faced numerous hardships and struggles in his early life. He dropped out of high school and was homeless for a period, living in abandoned buildings and surviving on the streets.

However, Eric's life took a turn when he encountered a mentor who helped him rediscover his purpose and potential. He went on to earn his GED, and later pursued higher education, eventually obtaining a Ph.D. in Education Administration. During his academic journey, Eric developed a deep passion for motivating and inspiring others.

Eric's unique style of blending motivational speaking with elements of hip-hop culture gained attention and attracted a growing audience. He started delivering powerful speeches that resonated with individuals seeking transformation and personal growth. Eric's message emphasized the importance of self-belief, hard work, and perseverance in achieving success.

Recognizing the significance of surrounding oneself with individuals who share similar goals, Eric formed a strong community of followers and supporters. He created platforms such as the "ET Inspires" YouTube channel, where he shares his motivational speeches, and established programs and events that bring together individuals from diverse backgrounds, united in their pursuit of personal and professional growth.

Through his speeches, books, and workshops, Eric Thomas has inspired countless individuals to believe in themselves and strive for greatness. His story exemplifies the power of joining forces with others who share similar goals, as the collective energy and support can propel individuals to achieve extraordinary results.

In Eric Thomas's own words, "When you want to succeed as badly as you want to breathe, then you'll be successful." His story serves as an inspiration to anyone facing adversity, reminding us that with determination, self-belief, and a supportive community, we can overcome obstacles and achieve our dreams.

It's essential for achieving success, fulfillment, and a sense of purpose in various aspects of life. Whether it's personal, professional, or social goals, connecting with like-minded individuals can provide valuable support, collaboration, learning, and a sense of community that can make a significant difference in your life.

Through your experiences, you came to believe what the people around you tell you. You can create your own world. As you progress, be inspired, and encouraged and find the answers within yourself to important questions, without depending on other people that don't have the same interests that you have. Continuing to grow is a challenging path to follow, you may struggle, and it might take time, but keep depending on you.

You may give into temptation several times on your journey but get back on track before it's too late. You could frame inspirational quotes and hang them around the house to remind yourself to keep on track with your goals. You cannot set a deadline for enlightenment, but you can realize it is your purpose in your life to strive and stay motivated. Unfortunately, you may not have the support of your family, because they don't understand or have the desires that you have.

I learned an easy way to stay motivated and be encouraged. I learned to be around like-minded people. People that have the same interests that I do. People that are aiming for the same desires that I have. People that want to have the same things as I do. Like they always say, birds of a feather flock together. My point is this, you want to be around people that are doing some of the same things you're doing. That way, you'll be around people that understand the obstacles you go through. Through networking, you can get some valuable solutions.

If you're a writer with a goal of getting published, you could join a writer's workshop. If you'd like to become a golf champion, join a golf club. An inspiring artist may want to live in an artist community for inspiration and support. Someone who wants to start their own podcast might want to join a social media community. An entrepreneur may want to join their nearest Chamber of Commerce. Someone wanting to become a hair stylist might become an intern at a hair salon.

Surround yourself with people who push you to do and be better. People with higher goals and higher motivation, good times, and positive energy, with no jealousy or hate. You all should bring out the best in one another. Finding people with the same goals will help supercharge your vision. Sometimes it's hard to achieve your vision alone. A group will help you achieve your vision, and you can help them achieve theirs as well.

You must strategically partner with other people that are going in the same direction as you are. Many people make a mistake and partner with people for the wrong reasons. Just because they have a positive impact on your life does not mean they're the right person for reaching your goals. A person that's not heading in the same direction as you and your goals can create conflict. You would then become frustrated with one another because you're not on the same page. When two people have different visions and are incompatible with each other, the relationship will suffer.

Action Steps

Find people with similar goals and partner with them today. Join some social media groups online in the field you wish to be in. Join your local Kiwanis Club. Go to your local council and commission meetings. Join your local Chamber of Commerce. Are you joining all the Clubs?

"There's no talent here, this is hard work. This is an obsession. Talent does not exist; we are all equal as human beings. You could be anyone if you put in the time. You will reach the top, and that's that. I am not talented, I'm obsessed." – Conor McGregor

31
Reward Yourself

Rewarding yourself can be an excellent way to celebrate your accomplishments, boost your motivation, and maintain your momentum towards your goals. Here are some ways you can reward yourself:

- **Treat yourself to a nice meal:** You can go out to your favorite restaurant or cook a special meal at home to celebrate your success.
- **Take a relaxing bath:** You can light some candles, add some essential oils, and take a long, hot bath to help you unwind and destress.
- **Go on a trip:** You can take a weekend getaway or plan a more extended vacation to a place you have always wanted to visit.
- **Buy something you have been wanting:** You can treat yourself to something you have had your eye on, such as a new outfit, a piece of jewelry, or a gadget.

- **Take a day off:** You can take a personal day from work or take a break from your routine to do something you enjoy, such as reading a book, watching a movie, or spending time with friends and family.

- **Try a new hobby:** You can use your reward as an opportunity to try a new hobby or activity you have been curious about, such as painting, photography, or hiking.

- **Schedule a spa day:** You can pamper yourself with a spa day, including a massage, facial, and other treatments.

- **Spend time in nature:** You can plan a day trip or weekend getaway to a national park, beach, or other natural area to enjoy the beauty of the outdoors.

- **Have a fun night out:** You can plan a night out with friends, such as going to a concert, comedy show, or sporting event.

- **Donate to a charity:** You can donate to a charity or volunteer for a cause that is meaningful to you as a way to give back and feel good about your success.

Mel Robbins is a renowned speaker, author, and life coach, known for her empowering and practical advice on personal and professional growth. Throughout her career, Mel has emphasized the significance of celebrating achievements and rewarding oneself as an essential part of the goal-setting process. However, her understanding of this principle didn't come easily.

Mel faced her own share of personal and professional challenges. At one point, she found herself in a difficult financial situation, struggling with anxiety and a lack of motivation. In her darkest moments, she realized that she needed to make a change and take control of her life.

Mel developed a transformative approach called "The 5 Second Rule," which involves taking action within five seconds to overcome self-doubt and procrastination. Through this technique, she began making positive changes, which ultimately led to her success as a speaker and author.

Along her journey, Mel recognized that celebrating milestones and rewarding herself played a crucial role in maintaining motivation and sustaining progress. She understood that acknowledging accomplishments, no matter how small, is a powerful way to reinforce positive behavior and build momentum.

Mel encourages individuals to establish a reward system that aligns with their personal preferences and values. Whether it's treating oneself to a small indulgence, taking a vacation, or simply enjoying a day off, she believes that incorporating rewards into the goal-setting process helps cultivate a positive mindset and drives future success.

By practicing what she preaches, Mel Robbins exemplifies the importance of self-care and self-appreciation in achieving personal and professional growth. She understands that acknowledging one's achievements, no matter how big or small, creates a positive cycle of motivation, self-belief, and continued progress.

Mel's story serves as a reminder that reaching goals is not solely about the end result but also the journey itself. By rewarding oneself along the way, individuals can stay motivated, sustain their momentum, and cultivate a sense of fulfillment and satisfaction.

In Mel Robbins' words, "The only way to change is to outdo yourself again and again. And the only way to do that is to celebrate when you do." Her story inspires us to celebrate our accomplishments and embrace self-reward as an integral part of the goal-setting process.

Rewarding yourself can be a great way to celebrate your accomplishments, recharge your batteries, and stay motivated towards your goals. There are many different ways to reward yourself, so choose what feels right for you and enjoy the process of treating yourself to something special.

Congratulations! There's no turning back now. You are an official G.O.A.L. Digga! You have completed this book challenge. You're now equipped with the tools you need for your new journey in life. It's time to celebrate! Go out, dance, dance, and dance! Let's GOOOOOOOOO!

Action Steps

Call up your friends and family and let them know that you are now available and ready to celebrate your accomplishments with them. Let them know that you appreciate their patience and support as you planned your journey, and you are continuing to grow. If you were on this journey by yourself, no worries, post it to your social media pages and don't forget to tag your G.O.A.L. Digga community. We are here for you.

"You will continue to suffer if you have an emotional reaction to everything that is said to you. True power is sitting back and observing everything with logic. If words can control you that means that everyone else can control you. Breathe and allow things to have." – Bruce Lee

BONUS: 51 Goals to Invest in Yourself

1. Set new goals.
2. Read 30 minutes a day.
3. Start a blog about your transformation.
4. Learn a new language.
5. Take a long walk or learn Yoga.
6. Write in your Journal daily.
7. Drink water every day.
8. Allow yourself to "relax".
9. Meet new friends.
10. Meditate every day.
11. Smile every day.
12. Turn your negative thoughts into positive solutions.
13. Do random acts of kindness.
14. Implement healthier eating habits.
15. Redecorate your room and living spaces.
16. Start your day with gratitude.
17. Write down daily affirmations.
18. Learn to play an instrument.

19. Plan a self-care day every month.

20. Clear your mind with a brain dump.

21. Create a digital product.

22. Write a book.

23. Keep a healing Crystal that wards off all bad energy and promotes wellness.

24. Make a bucket list.

25. Do one thing that brings you out of your comfort zone.

26. Wake up an hour earlier each day.

27. Talk to a transformational coach.

28. Buy a nice outfit that makes you feel good.

29. Join a workshop of your favorite hobby.

30. Join a social club.

31. Complete a challenge.

32. Start a garden.

33. Let go of toxic relationships.

34. Get rid of bad habits.

35. Learn a new skill.

36. Plan a trip out of state or country.

37. Forgive yourself for past mistakes.

38. Let go of any animosity you have for others.

39. Plan your monthly budget.

40. Get rid of clutter in your workspace and living space.

41. Get a makeover to go with your new hairstyle.

42. Set boundaries.

43. Adopt a pet.

44. Start a business.

45. Create a vision board.

46. Document your life.

47. Love yourself.

48. Go Hiking or bike riding.

49. Volunteer for a cause you love.

50. Learn to say no.

51. Get a Mentor.

Congratulations you are now a certified G.O.A.L.

Digga!

About the Author

Myra Sirrene is a self-made success story, rising some challenging beginnings to become a successful influencer, entrepreneur, and thought leader. Born into poverty, Sirrene faced numerous challenges throughout her life, including homelessness, depression, and low self-esteem. Despite these obstacles she remained determined and focused on her goals, driven by a deep desire to provide a better life for her family.

Over the years, Sirrene has accomplished more than most people even dream of. She has built several successful businesses, created multiple streams of income through products and services, and has become a highly respected influencer in her field. Her achievements have been recognized by many, and she has received numerous accolades for her work, including becoming the RPE Alabama Chapter President of a prestigious online Financial Literacy University.

But what sets Sirrene apart is her unwavering commitment to giving back. Despite her success, she remains humble, deeply connected to her roots, and is passionate about helping others who face similar challenges. She is an active philanthropist and community leader, using her influence and resources to support causes that she believes in.

Today, Sirrene continues to inspire and motivate others through her writing, speaking engagement, and social media channels. She shares her life experiences, insights, and strategies for success, in the hope of empowering others to achieve their full potential.

Sirrene is a true testament to the power of perseverance, determination, and hard work. Her story is a source of inspiration for anyone who has ever faced adversity and believes that success was out of reach. She proves that with planning, dedication, and a positive mindset, anything is possible.